J.L.E.
152-154 Golders Green Road
London NW11 8HE

The Torah
RESOURCES CENTRE

FREE LENDING LIBRARY

"Sweeten the words of Your Torah in our mouth and in the mouth of Your people."

Shacharis Torah Blessings

Dedicated to the memory of Rivka Henna bat Yissachar and Leib ben Pinchas King ע"ה

Please 'log out' this book before borrowing it.

If found, please call 0181 907 5021 or

....

Please take good care of this book.

© 1995. TRC

JLE BOOK & AUDIO CLUB

- Please return by the latest date stamped below to avoid a charge.

- May not be renewed if required by another reader.

book & audio club

152-154 Golders Green Road
London NW11 8HE
Tel: 0181 458 4588

היסטוריה

The ArtScroll History Series®

Rabbis Nosson Scherman / Meir Zlotowitz
General Editors

FROM KLETZK

by
Rabbi Alter Pekier

Edited by Gertrude Hirschler

TO SIBERIA

A yeshivah bachur's wanderings during the Holocaust

Published by

Mesorah Publications, ltd

FIRST EDITION
First Impression ... March, 1985

Published and Distributed by
MESORAH PUBLICATIONS, Ltd.
Brooklyn, New York 11223

Distributed in Israel by
MESORAH MAFITZIM / J. GROSSMAN
Rechov Harav Uziel 117
Jerusalem, Israel

Distributed in Europe by
J. LEHMANN HEBREW BOOKSELLERS
20 Cambridge Terrace / Gateshead
Tyne and Wear / England NE8 1RP

ARTSCROLL HISTORY SERIES®
FROM KLETZK TO SIBERIA
© Copyright 1985 by MESORAH PUBLICATIONS, Ltd.
1969 Coney Island Avenue / Brooklyn, N.Y. 11223 / (718) 339-1700

ALL RIGHTS RESERVED.
This text, the new translation and commentary and introductions,
including the typographic layout and cover artwork,
have been designed, edited and revised as to content, form and style.

No part of this book may be reproduced **in any form**
without **written** permission from the copyright holder,
except by a reviewer who wishes to quote brief passages
in connection with a review written for inclusion in magazines or newspapers.

THE RIGHTS OF THE COPYRIGHT HOLDER WILL BE STRICTLY ENFORCED.

ISBN: 0-89906-470-1 (hard cover)
0-89906-471-X (paperback)

Typography by CompuScribe at ArtScroll Studios, Ltd.
1969 Coney Island Avenue / Brooklyn, N.Y. 11223 / (718) 339-1700
Printed and bound in the United States of America

❦ Table of Contents

Foreword *by Rabbi Pinchas M. Teitz*	*vii*
Introduction	*ix*
The Last Summer	15
War	18
Days of Awe, 5700	22
Vilna: October, 1939 — February, 1940	28
Yanova: February — August, 1940	37
Reb Aharon Leaves	45
The Yeshivah Breaks Camp	52
The Long Journey East	57
Labor Camp Number Seven: June — October, 1941	63
Farewell to Siberia	77
The Jews of Chymkent	86
Living as Jews in a Kolkhoz	89
Passover in Mankent: 1942	95
Sorrows and Joys	100
My Wedding	106
We Leave the Soviet Paradise	114
Lodz	120
Postwar Anti-Semitism	124
My Search for the Fischermans	127
Distinguished Visitors	129
Exodus from Poland	133
Prague	136
Paris and London	145
Ellis Island	152
Irving Bunim	155

~§ Foreword

After four decades of silence, Jewry throughout the world has suddenly awakened to the realization that an unforgivable national offense is being committed by neglecting the gathering of testimony concerning the events that transpired during the Holocaust years of 1940-45.

It has taken forty years for our people to realize their responsibility for averting the possibility of archenemies of Jewry completely denying, minimizing or belittling the most horrible brutalities ever perpetrated against any nation. Indeed, we witness today a concerted effort orchestrated by שונאי ישראל to deny the occurrence of the tragedy witnessed by the whole world, the annihilation of a third of the Jewish nation.

Perhaps the long delay in recognizing this responsibility may be found in the Talmudic statement that לא קאי איניש אדעתיה דרביה עד ארבעין שנין (*Avodah Zarah* 5b) — the proper perspective towards an historical event, and the lessons to be derived therefrom, may not be obtained until forty years have elapsed.

In the merciless and virtually total destruction of Jewish life in Eastern Europe, a remnant of Torah comprising several hundred students of the great European yeshivos was miraculous preserved. This remnant consisted of two groups. One, the renowned Mirrer Yeshivah, proceeded in its totality to Shanghai, China. The other, students of famous Polish yeshivos, spent the war years in Siberia.

One of the latter group, Rabbi Moshe Pekier שליט״א, a Talmudic scholar of note, recorded his memoirs of the experiences endured in *Galus* Siberia. On the one hand, his talented pen gives the reader a graphic description of the tribulations and agonies that were the lot of the exiles. On the other hand, the deep and abiding faith and determination by which these trials were surmounted permeates his words.

His book is a great contribution to Jewish and Torah history, and should be required reading not only for the student of Jewish history seeking first-hand documentation of the events recorded therein, but for the Torah world was well, to learn the extent to which dedication to Torah ideals can extend even under the most adverse conditions.

May השי"ת grant Rabbi Pekier many more productive years in the field of Torah and *Yiras Shomayim*.

Rabbi Pinchas M. Teitz
Elizabeth, N.J.

ABOUT THE AUTHOR

Rabbi Moshe Chaim (Alter) Pekier was born in Slutzk, Russia, at the end of World War I. Upon the Communist takeover, his family joined many other Jews fleeing across the border to nearby Kletzk, Poland. It was there that Alter Pekier was raised in close proximity to the famed yeshivah of Rabbi Aharon Kotler, who became his revered mentor. With the exception of two years in Kamenetz under Rabbi Boruch Ber Lebovitz, Rabbi Pekier studied in Kletzk until the period described in this book.

After the war, he rejoined Rabbi Kotler for four years of study in Lakewood, New Jersey, where he was ordained by the Rosh Yeshivah. He served for two years as rabbi of Congregation Midrash Eliyahu, in the East New York section of Brooklyn. Then began an illustrious 31-year career as Talmudic lecturer in the prestigious West Side Institutional Synagogue in Manhattan, from which he retired with honors in January, 1983. He serves on the boards of various rabbinic and educational organizations.

The Pekiers have a son and four daughters, all raising distinguished scholarly families in the tradition of their parents.

~§ Introduction

"Remember the days of old, consider the years of each generation" (*Deuteronomy* 32:7).

These two Biblical statements: "Remember the days of old," and "consider the years of each generation," are closely linked with one another. The Torah bids us to remember the days of yore with all its happenings, both happy and sad, with all its successes and failures. Only by learning from the past is it possible to evaluate all the experiences of the present, to put the present in the proper perspective and to live a life of *Kiddush Hashem* [Sanctification of the Name], a life that brings honor to the Name of G-d in the present-day world.

Siberia is a vast expanse of land covering over five million square miles, stretching from the Ural Mountains to the Pacific Ocean, and from the Arctic Ocean to Mongolia and Manchuria. Siberia is rich in copper, zinc, lead, coal, gold and uranium, yet it is one of the world's most poorly developed regions, due partly to its harsh climate — torrid summers alternating with frigid winters — but in an even larger measure to the economic system under which its twenty million inhabitants must live. Communist Russia, offering its workers little incentive and compensation for their toil, has never been able to exploit Siberia's natural resources efficiently. As a result, much of the wealth G-d gave to that subcontinent still lies buried in the ground.

The Soviet government did, however, enrich Siberia with one resource known throughout the world: hundreds of concentration camps where the best of Russia's sons and daughters have been kept in isolation and at hard labor by a system that has branded them as potential traitors. Among the exiles and slave laborers who passed through Siberia during the years of the Nazi Holocaust were tens of thousands of Jews, mostly from Poland and Lithuania. Among these were hundreds of yeshivah students who had been snatched from the sheltering warmth of the yeshivah atmosphere and deported deep into Asiatic Russia for no other reason but that they refused to exchange G-d and His Torah for the teachings of Marx and Lenin. I was one of those yeshivah students.

It was a tragedy for anyone to be exiled to Siberia, hundreds of miles from civilization, where few outsiders ever came. But for us yeshivah *bachurim*, who had spent virtually all our conscious lives in the diligent study of the Torah and who had been nurtured in Jewish communities that looked to the great yeshivos of Poland and Lithuania for their spiritual survival, this banishment was catastrophic, both physically and spiritually.

Some of my classmates died of sickness or starvation and were buried in the woods of Siberia or — later — in the deserts of Kazakhstan. But with the help of the Almighty, most of us survived these six years of incredible hardship and anguish, and we returned to the free Jewish world whole in body, mind and spirit. We feel that our survival has placed upon us the responsibility to record our story for our children and grandchildren so that they may better appreciate the freedom in which they can devote their energies to the study and the furtherance of Torah today.

Forty years have passed since our liberation from Siberia and Kazakhstan. Yet, the story of our unique exile and our wanderings halfway across the world has remained largely unknown, even to those of our fellow Jews whose own spiritual development was eventually shaped by scholars and students from our group. Many of us believe that if our years of exile, which became the predominant influence in our formative years, were to be forgotten, it would be an irretrievable loss to Jewish history.

In the summer of 1982, while vacationing in the Catskill Mountains, where many scholars and students of the "yeshivah world" may be found during the summer months, I searched my memory for the events, times and places that represent the milestones of my years in Asiatic Russia. Thanks to the Almighty, I was able to recall and to gather enough material for this small book.

Initially, I had intended it only for my own children and grandchildren, but friends who read my manuscript encouraged me to have it published for a larger audience.

My story first appeared in Yiddish, in a series of articles in the popular Orthodox weekly *Der Algemeiner Journal*. I was surprised and pleased by the numerous letters and telephone calls I subsequently received, not only from people who, like myself, had spent the Holocaust years in Asiatic Russia, but also from others who had never heard of these events before.

At the urging of many friends and students I then set about to put these articles into book form and to have them translated into English.

The translation is the work of my daughter, Rochel, who took time from her many responsibilities as a wife, mother and teacher for this purpose, and her husband, Rabbi Meyer Yosef Portnoy. The original English manuscript was then typed by my youngest daughter, Shulamis, and her husband, Rabbi Yitzchok Zev Rubinfeld. To all of them, my gratitude and the prayerful wish that the Almighty may reward them for their devotion.

For valued editorial suggestions and counsel, I am indebted to Miss Gertrude Hirschler, translator and editor of numerous works of classic Torah literature.

I wish to express my deep-felt gratitude to my wife Rivka, my loyal, devoted helpmate who stands by my side in all my endeavors.

To the Portnoys and the Rubinfelds, and to my other children, Rabbi Levi Pekier and his wife, Leah; Rabbi Yosef Yitzchok and Chaya Strassfeld; and Rabbi Moshe Yeshaya and Cheni Gitelis, as well as to my grandchildren, my thanks for the inspiration they have given me through their own dedication to Torah and their eagerness to follow in the hallowed footsteps of their forebears.

And of course, *odeh es Hashem b'chol levov*, I thank the Almighty with all my heart for granting me life and health to complete this record of the adversities and the miracles I have witnessed, and for helping me to understand, through my own experience, that one must never lose one's hope and faith in the help and guidance of the One Above.

Alter Pekier

Shevat 5745/February 1985
New York, New York

FROM KLETZK TO SIBERIA

The Last Summer

THE SPRING OF 1939 began as usual in our hometown, Kletzk. The sun shone brightly over the slanted roofs of the wooden houses that lined the narrow streets. The flowers that poked their heads from the winter soil added gay touches of color to the ordinary drab scene of the Jewish quarter. Young people passed through the cobbled streets with quickened steps and happy smiles. That spring, like all other springtimes, stirred dreams and hopes that had lain dormant all winter long.

Yet there was in Kletzk an undercurrent of tension, even anxiety. The very air smelled of war, because Nazi Germany was stretching its greedy fingers toward Poland. Hitler's propaganda machine bombarded the Poles with ceaseless threats and warnings. We knew it was only a matter of time before the Germans would attack.

My younger brother Berl and I were students at the famous Etz Chaim Yeshivah of Kletzk, whose head was Reb Aharon Kotler, that giant of Torah scholarship whom we lovingly called "Reb Aharon." I was twenty-one; Berl was eighteen. We yeshivah *bachurim* that summer were perhaps among the first to realize the seriousness of the political situation, because many of our classmates who previously had been exempt from military duty suddenly received draft notices from the Polish army. And one day our "American" student, Reb Gedalia Schorr, a young man in his late twenties who had come to Kletzk from Brooklyn,

Faculty and student body of Yeshivah Etz Chaim of Kletzk, 1938

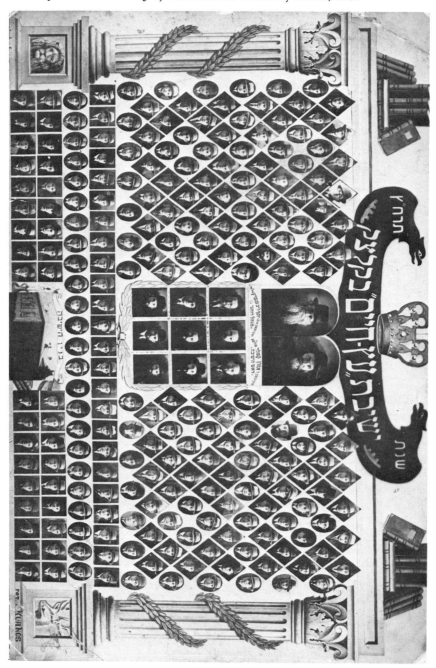

16 / FROM KLETZK TO SIBERIA

New York, with his young bride only ten months earlier, was advised by the American consulate in Warsaw to return home as soon as possible because of the danger of war. And so Reb Gedalia, who had intended to study at Kletzk for five years, and his wife, Shifra, took the first boat back to New York.

That summer the hatred of the Poles for the Jews, which had never been far from the surface, reached new heights. Young *Endeks*, hooligans from the notoriously anti-Semitic Polish Nationalist party, now not only attacked Jews in the streets but also broke into their homes. Instead of devoting their efforts to preparing for the struggle against Nazi Germany, these primitive, ignorant Poles wasted their energies on harassing their Jewish neighbors, loyal citizens who had contributed substantially to Poland's prosperity since the founding of the Polish Republic in 1918.

In addition to physical and psychological persecution, the Jews of Poland suffered economic abuse. The Polish government floated a *pozichka narodova*, a compulsory loan to cover the costs of the anticipated war. Every citizen was forced by law to participate in this loan but in the case of the Jews the government arbitrarily set the sum of money that each individual had to contribute, without regard to his financial capabilities. My father

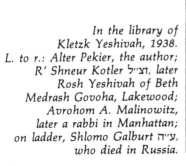

In the library of Kletzk Yeshivah, 1938. L. to r.: Alter Pekier, the author; R' Shneur Kotler זצ"ל, later Rosh Yeshivah of Beth Medrash Govoha, Lakewood; Avrohom A. Malinowitz, later a rabbi in Manhattan; on ladder, Shlomo Galburt ה"י, who died in Russia.

THE LAST SUMMER / 17

was asked for an amount far in excess of his personal assets. Luckily, generous friends helped him meet the government's demands so that he did not have to go to prison.

Meanwhile, military maneuvers were held in the vicinity of Kletzk with infantry, cavalry and artillery units all taking part. As we watched these woefully untrained soldiers and puny tanks play their war games, we realized that if and when the Germans attacked, Poland would collapse at once. Only our Father in heaven could save us now.

War

ON THURSDAY, August 24, 1939, the world learned that Joachim von Ribbentrop, the German foreign minister, had flown to Moscow. The exact purpose of his journey to the Soviet Union was not divulged, but it was generally understood that the chief topic of Ribbentrop's discussions with Prime Minister Viacheslav Molotov would be the future of Poland.

There was an immediate mobilization of all young and middle-aged men, and the streets of Kletzk were soon filled with soldiers and new recruits. Each day we saw men in uniform parting from their wives, their children and their aged parents, all weeping bitterly because they feared that they would never see each other again.

The Polish government set up a forced labor camp near Kletzk for those suspected of disloyalty, mostly Communist sympathizers or holders of Nansen passports. Issued by the League of Nations to "legitimize" the stateless refugees created by World War I, these documents did nothing for the stateless Jews in Poland. My father, who had fled to Poland from territory occupied by Soviet Russia after 1918, had a Nansen passport, but instead of guaranteeing our security, it only stamped our family as people without a country. Each time there was a knock at our door, we were terrified that it might be the police and that my father, my brother Berl, and I would be taken be taken to the labor camp. Luckily my father was known as a quiet, law-abiding citizen who never involved himself in politics. And so he was not interned, nor were we. In fact, our father's Nansen passport eventually gave my brother Berl and me a special advantage; unlike many of our draft-age friends who were Polish citizens, Berl and I, as "foreigners," were not inducted into the army. My brother Mordechai was still too young to be subject to the draft.

The Kletzk study in the summer of 1939. At the lower right is Alter Pekier

The Rosh Yeshivah, Rabbi Aharon Kotler
זכר צדיק לברכה

The Downfall of Poland

ON FRIDAY MORNING, September 1, we woke to panic-stricken announcements on the radio repeating over and over again, "Germany has attacked our homeland! German plans are bombing military installations in Warsaw, Cracow and other cities!" These reports were laced with military marches and other patriotic music, ostensibly to bolster public morale.

The mood among the *bachurim* at our yeshivah was of unrelieved gloom. Many had already received their draft notices; those who had not, expected to be called at any moment. That Friday afternoon, before *minchah* services, the Rosh Yeshivah Reb Aharon Kotler delivered a *mussar shmuss*, a talk on Jewish laws on ethic and moral conduct. He urged us to repent of our past sins and to pray for Hitler's downfall, the safety of the Jews, and survival of all decent people everywhere in the struggle against the common enemy. As he spoke, tears streamed down his cheeks. We, his disciples, wept with him.

The Torah portion read in the synagogue on the next day included the curses that had been pronounced in the wilderness upon those children of Israel who sinned against the commandments of G-d. As the reader intoned the curses, one by one, we prayed that they would fall not upon us but upon the Germans and their allies.

The next day — Sunday, September 3 — England and France declared war on Germany. We were relieved, almost happy again, because we felt sure that Germany could not fight on two fronts at the same time.

Each evening I reported to Reb Aharon the communiques I had heard on the radio that day. At first, there were encouraging reports of Polish forces holding their positions in the north and repelling German onslaughts on the southern front. But one night, after I had given him a particularly optimistic summary of the day's military developments, Reb Aharon asked me whether the commentator had singled out any front-line towns or cities for special mention. Yes, I replied: Bidgoz on the northern front and Radom in the south. In that case, said Reb Aharon, the situation must be deteriorating. Since these two places had not been mentioned in the previous day's news, it was clear to him that within the twenty-four hours just past, the Poles had been forced to retreat to positions farther inland. Alas, our Rosh Yeshivah's interpretation turned out to be correct.

Days of Awe, 5700

DURING THE FIRST WEEKS of war, refugees from all over Poland streamed into Kletzk. They came from Warsaw, Lodz, Cracow and other cities that were either within range of German artillery or already in the hands of the Germans.

By Rosh HaShanah, 1939, less than two weeks after the German invasion had begun, Poland was virtually on her knees. All the large cities in the central region, except for Warsaw, had been occupied by the German army. Many Polish regiments had already surrendered to the Germans, and the highways were jammed with Polish deserters fleeing for their lives.

On that Rosh HaShanah — September 14 and 15, 1939 — we recited our prayers with more fervor than ever before, because we saw our lives hanging in the balance. We felt that one word, one act on our part could tip the scales of G-d's justice either way and decide our fate. On the second day of Rosh HaShanah the Germans bombed the town of Baranovice, very near Kletzk. By that evening, Kletzk was filled with refugees from Baranovice.

ON SEPTEMBER 17, the Sunday before Yom Kippur, I got up very early in the morning to attend *selichos* services at the yeshivah. The streets were deserted; most of the gentile townspeople were still asleep. And then a strange and unexpected thing happened. A long line

Soviet Russia Occupies Eastern Poland

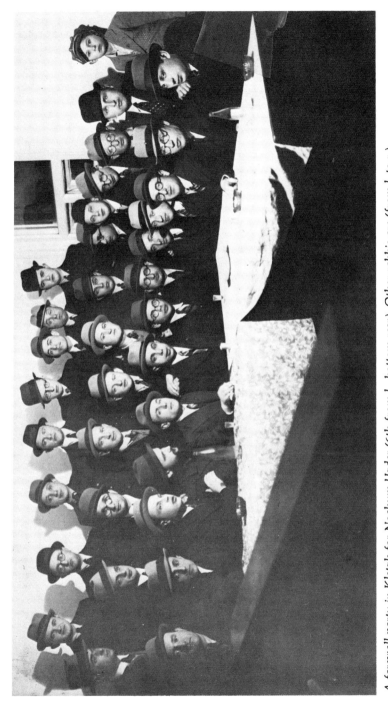

A farewell party in Kletzk for Nochum Uzder (6th from l., bottom row). Other rabbis are (from l. to r.) middle row: 7th, Shaul Goldman, Brooklyn; 9th, Shmuel Maslow, Brooklyn; 12th, Leib Polak, Denver; top row: 1st, Yaakov Zaretzky, Bnei Brak; 5th, R' Shneur Kotler ל״זצ, Lakewood; 8th, Alter Pekier of soldiers, their horses and wagons piled high with weapons, came marching down Zepfer Street and headed for the market place. To my surprise, I saw that these were Russian troops. Later, I learned that the Russians had crossed Poland's eastern border about half an hour earlier without meeting any Polish resistance. And so they were now in Kletzk, only six kilometers from the border, and moving on toward Baranovice.

The arrival of the Soviets was the result of the agreement that had been signed between von Ribbentrop and Molotov in Moscow one week before the German attack on Poland. Soviet Russia and Nazi Germany had divided Poland between themselves. Germany was to get the central and western sectors, while Russia received the eastern part. The Russians had waited for more than two weeks before claiming their share, hoping that, in the meantime, German bombs would crush all Polish resistance so that the Red Army could move in without suffering any casualties.

By midmorning Kletzk was filled with noise and confusion. The Jews cheered the Russians as their liberators from Polish Fascism, which had made anti-Semitism an official policy between the two World Wars. The *shechitah* had been restricted, making it almost impossible for observant Jews to obtain meat. There had been *ovsham* or boycotts against all Jewish business, and pogroms had taken place in many cities.

Now the Jews of Kletzk gathered in small groups, discussing the new situation. How would Russian occupation affect their lives? One man reported that he had seen the mayor of the town, a notorious Jew-baiter, seized by Russian soldier and taken away, under arrest, in an armored car. Though it was clear that life under Communist rule would be far from ideal and that the future was uncertain, many Jews felt relieved that they had been saved, at least for the moment, from falling into the hands of the Nazis.

The gentiles, on the other hand, were dismayed and badly frightened. And as usual, they vented their anger and frustration on the Jews. A young yeshivah student was grabbed by a gang of

Student body of the Yeshivah crowded around Reb Aharon to hear his shiur.

Poles and forced, at gunpoint, to remove a figure of Jesus from a church. Meanwhile, the Communist youth, suddenly promoted from "illegals" to "guardians of law and order," came out of hiding; they marched through the streets with rifles given them by the Russians and happily distributed tobacco to anyone they saw.

The Yeshivah

BUT THE STUDENTS at the yeshivah could not find it in their hearts to rejoice. Eighteen years earlier, in 1921, Reb Aharon Kotler and his disciples had been forced to flee from the Russians in Slutzk and to re-establish their yeshivah in Kletzk. And now Reb Aharon and his yeshivah *bachurim* found themselves face to face with the Communists once again.

However, we had no time for wailing and hand-wringing. The yeshivah had to continue its life under the new realities. No matter what befell them, the 200 *bachurim* had to eat. Food had to be obtained and stored to see us through the winter. The peasants in the area, certain that most of their land would be confiscated, offered us the remnants of their vegetable crops as gifts, under the condition that we harvest the produce ourselves.

And so, every morning, we yeshivah *bachurim* went out to the fields with hired horses and wagons. In the evening, we returned to the yeshivah with wagonloads of potatoes, carrots, onions and cucumbers. The peasants were glad to be rid of it, and the yeshivah was certainly happy to get it. The Jewish merchants in town provided the yeshivah with flour, sugar, salt, cheese and other staple foods in return for our promise that they would receive nominal payments when conditions returned to normal. As a result, we were able to gather an ample supply of food, enough to last us at least until the end of the year.

Nevertheless, our prayers during the Days of Penitence and on Yom Kippur were heavy with tears as we pleaded with G-d not to abandon us during the difficult days to come. But when the festival of Sukkos followed the solemn High Holidays, we did our best not to let the uncertain present mar the celebration of the "season of our joy." We sang and danced, and we recited the blessing over the *lulav* and *esrog* as we did every year, except that this year there was only one *lulav* and one *esrog* from the entire yeshivah. That *lulav* and *esrog* had been sent to Reb Aharon from Eretz Yisrael shortly before the outbreak of the war by his father-in-law, the renowned Rav Isser Zalman Meltzer, head of the Yeshivah Etz Chaim in Jerusalem.

On Shemini Atzeres and Simchas Torah the prayer hall of our yeshivah resounded with happy songs and the thump of dancing feet as the *bachurim* and the other Jews of Kletzk rejoiced in the Torah. The Soviet occupation authorities heard the commotion and probably did not like it, but they did nothing to disturb us.

Roshei Yeshivah Meet in Vilna

ON THE DAY AFTER the holidays Reb Aharon received a telegram from Reb Chaim Ozer Grodzensky in Vilna, asking him to come to Vilna at once for an important meeting. Reb Chaim Ozer was widely known not only as an outstanding Torah scholar but also as a wise leader to whom Jews from the world over turned with their religious and social problems. He now convened a conference of roshei yeshivah from the eastern sector of Poland to discuss ways of saving their yeshivos from almost certain liquidation by the Soviet authorities.

Reb Aharon left for Vilna the next morning, Sunday, October 8, 1939. He never returned to Kletzk. On the following Wednesday evening, October 11, his wife, Rebbetzin Chana Perel Kotler, received a telegram from him, asking her, their son and daughter, and the entire yeshivah to leave Kletzk at once and to join him in Vilna. This had been the decision made by Reb Chaim Ozer in consultation with the other roshei yeshivah.

My brother Berl and I did not understand why Reb Aharon should consider Vilna safer for us than Kletzk. Vilna had once been the capital of Lithuania, but now, like Kletzk, it was under Soviet occupation. However, we were accustomed to regard any wish of the Rosh Yeshivah as our command, for we had not only profound respect for his great scholarship but also implicit trust in his practical good sense.

Before long we were to see that Reb Chaim Ozer Grodzensky and Reb Aharon Kotler had made the right decision.

Vilna: October, 1939 — February, 1940

WHEN POLAND LOST the war with Russia in 1795, she also lost her independence. For 123 years, until 1918, the end of World War I, what had once been Poland was divided among Germany, Austria and Russia. When Poland became an independent country again after World War I, she expected to get Vilna and its suburbs, which had been Polish territory for twenty-three years from 1772 to 1795. But the Poles were bitterly disappointed for Russia turned Vilna over to Lithuania, on the grounds that the Lithuanians had historical claims to that territory since it had been theirs for many years before 1772. Furious at this diabolical plot, Poland did not accept the plan, but sent an army directed by General Zeligovsky to reclaim Vilna. After a short fight Poland regained Vilna and integrated it into Poland. In the angry aftermath of this battle, in the years between the world wars, Poland and Lithuania remained officially at war. There was no mail or other communications between them.

During World War II, when Soviet Russia occupied eastern Poland, it surprisingly declared its willingness to return Vilna to Lithuania. We yeshivah students were certain that the Soviets, by doing this, were only furthering their evil ambitions and that this magnanimity would not last long. Unfortunately, time proved us right. In the new status of Vilna as a Lithuanian city not under Russian control, we recognized the hand of G-d, enabling our yeshivah students, as well as other religious Jews to escape the Communist regime. Realizing the possibility of our fleeing to the free world, when Lithuania would take over Vilna, the roshei yeshivah decided and subsequently demanded that all students head for Vilna.

We Leave Kletzk

IT WAS CLEAR from Reb Aharon's telegraph that he expected us to leave Kletzk within twenty-four hours. As we gathered our belongings, we were torn by mixed emotions. On the one hand, we hoped that our move to Vilna would be our first step to freedom. On the other hand, Berl and I, and many of the other *bachurim*, had parents and families in Kletzk who would not be able to leave with us.

I remember weeping all that day, knowing that Berl and I might never see Kletzk, our parents, our brother Mordechai and our two sisters, Rochel and Shulamis, again. Our parents attempted to control their emotions, not wishing to add to our burden of sorrow. They recalled how they themselves had been forced to part with their parents less than twenty years earlier, fleeing from Slutzk in the wake of the Russian revolution. The victorious Bolsheviks, eager to rid themselves of "bourgeois" elements, had thrown Jewish "capitalists" into prison or deported them to Siberia. My father had been on the list of prominent Slutzk merchants marked for arrest. That was why my family had left Slutzk, where I had been born, and resettled in Kletzk, along with Reb Aharon and his yeshivah. Our mother still remembered the tearful farewells, for everyone knew that the Jews who chose to remain in Slutzk had given up their last chance of leaving the Soviet Union. Among those who had stayed behind were Mother's own parents, who felt too old and frail to withstand the rigors of flight and the hardships of starting life anew in another place.

Now, in the fall of 1939, history seemed to be repeating

Reb Levi and Cherna Reiza Pekier in 1915, shortly after their marriage

itself. Our parents spent the day before our departure packing enough food and clothing to see Berl and me through the journey and whatever might follow. That evening a caravan of horse-drawn wagons drew up at the yeshivah to take the *bachurim* and Reb Aharon's family to Baranovice, from where we were to take a train to Vilna. One of the wagons was reserved for Rebbetzin Kotler, her son Reb Yosef Chaim Shneur Kotler (known simply as "Reb Shneur") and her daughter Sarah, who was then still single.

When the moment of parting came, our parents could no longer restrain their feelings. My mother's sobs were so heartbreaking that I was sure her cries would penetrate the very heavens and force the hand of the Almighty. The Kletzk *bachurim* wept, and so did the boys from other places who

*Rabbi Shneur Kotler when he was Rosh Yeshivah
of Beth Medrash Govoha, Lakewood, New Jersey*

already knew that their hometowns had been captured by the Germans.

We Arrive in Baranovice

BARANOVICE WAS NOT FAR from Kletz, but traffic on the highway was so heavy with refugees and Polish troops that it took our wagons all night to make the journey. We arrived in Baranovice on Friday morning.

At the Baranovice railroad station we found utter chaos. People scurried about, not knowing what to do or where to go. The reports we heard from Vilna were anything but encouraging. It seemed that Vilna, well behind the battle zone, had become an island of refuge for Jews from all over Poland. As a result, there was a severe shortage of food and housing and we were advised that if we did not want to starve, we had better not go to Vilna.

We met a girl from Kletzk, Fanny Tabatchnik, who had been studying at the University of Vilna. She was now waiting for the next train home to Kletzk because the situation in Vilna had become, as she put it, "catastrophic."

After a brief consultation with Rebbetzin Kotler, we decided to send a telegram to Reb Aharon in Vilna, asking whether he still felt that we should join him. Then we went into town and prepared to spend Shabbos in Baranovice, because we were certain that Reb Aharon's reply would not come until after the Sabbath. Most of us had friends in Baranovice who agreed to extend their hospitality to us for the day.

Then, only one hour before the Sabbath began, we received word from the Rosh Yeshivah that we must not wait until after Shabbos but should leave for Vilna at once. We knew that if Reb Aharon instructed us to travel on the Sabbath, he must have reason to believe that our lives would be in danger if we stayed in Baranovice. And so we unpacked some of our food supplies right there at the station, recited *Kiddush*, ate a quick Sabbath meal (since fasting is forbidden on the Sabbath), then picked up our baggage and hurried to board the Vilna train, which pulled out of the station only moments later.

Aboard the train, in our car, we found the revered *"Tzemach Dovid,"* Rosh Yeshivah of Baranovice. He, too, was going to Vilna even though it was already Shabbos.

Vilna

WE ARRIVED IN VILNA at eight o'clock the next morning, Saturday, October 14. We stayed in the railroad terminal for the rest of the day. Now that we had reached safety, it was no longer permissible for us to travel on the Sabbath.

After the Sabbath had ended, the Ganeles brothers, two boys from Vilna who had studied with us at Kletzk but had returned home immediately after the outbreak of the war, appeared at the station. They bade us a hearty welcome and immediately began making arrangements for our lodging. This was not a simple task, because there were two hundred of us!

The rumors we had heard about the situation in Vilna did not seem to deter other Jewish refugees. To our surprise, our sister Rochel, a graduate of the Beth Jacob Teachers Seminary of Cracow (she was then nineteen), also came to Vilna. Our parents had let her go because conditions in Kletzk had become unbearable, as she told us. She was assigned a bed in a refugee shelter set up in a building near the railroad station, on Kiyavska Street, for Beth Jacob students and other Orthodox girls who had come to Vilna without their families.

Jews from every part of Soviet-occupied Poland poured into

In Vilna, 1940, from l. to r. Alter, Rochel הי"ד, and Dov Berl Pekier זצ"ל

Vilna. They came by train, by car and on foot. We met students from all the great yeshivos of Lithuania and central Poland — Mir, Kamenetz, Radin, Grodno, Bialystok and Mezhirich. Also among the refugees were such prominent communal leaders as Senator Trockenheim and Congressman Leibel Mintzberg, who had represented organized Orthodox Jewry in the Polish parliament, and the religious journalists David Flinker and Yeushson. To all these people, Vilna was a springboard from which they hoped to escape to Palestine, America or any other free country, anywhere

The 38th Anniversary celebration of Tiferes Bachurim in 1940. At the head of the table (א) is Rabbi Y. Feivelson.

in the world, that would accept them.

The students of the Kletzk yeshivah were given "learning space" at the Yogiches Beth HaMedrash, where we tried to recapture the zeal and concentration with which we had studied in Kletzk. We got our midday dinner each day at a public soup kitchen operated by the Jewish community of Vilna. Breakfast and supper came from the warm-hearted Jewish families who took us into their homes and whose compassion made the separation from our families a little easier to bear.

Berl and I stayed with Reb Shmerel Sharafan and his wife. Although their tiny apartment barely had room for them and their two daughters, these wonderful people willingly shared their home with Berl, myself and three yeshivah students from Bialystok.

Reb Shmerel was a well-known personality in Jewish Vilna. On longer winter Friday nights, he delivered lectures to *Tiferes Bachurim*, a group of Orthodox young men, on the Torah portion of the week. His lectures drew large audiences and were widely discussed throughout the week that followed. His kindness and personal charm will be long remembered by those who were privileged to listen to his learned discourses and to enjoy the

*A gathering in 1940 at the home of Reb Shmerel Sharafan.
Seated from l. to r.: Mordechai Wenger ז״ל, Michel Surasky הי״ד, unknown,
Reb Shmerel Sharafan הי״ד, Shimon Surasky ז״ל, Yaakov Feinberg הי״ד.
Standing: Miss Sharafan הי״ד, Alter Pekier, Feige Sharafan הי״ד,
Mrs. Sharafan הי״ד, Rochel Pekier הי״ד, Berl Pekier ז״ל*

hospitality of his home.

Only a few days after our arrival, we saw how wise Reb Aharon had been to insist that we come to Vilna. Soviet Russia announced her intention to return Vilna to Lithuania. So we would be under the jurisdiction of a neutral country, safe, it seemed, from both Nazi Germany and Communist Russia — at least temporarily.

WE COUNTED THE DAYS until the Lithuanians would take possession of Vilna. The date for the official takeover was set for Saturday, October 28. That Sabbath morning, two weeks to the day since our arrival, we *davened* with the early *minyan*, quickly ate our Sabbath dinner and hurried into the street to watch the Lithuanian troops enter the city.

The Lithuanians Are Coming

At exactly twelve noon, the ringing of church bells gave the signal for the proceedings to begin. The parade started with police on motorcycles, followed by Lithuanian infantry, cavalry and artillery units. There were so many soldiers that we wondered

VILNA: OCTOBER, 1939 – FEBRUARY, 1940 / 35

whether there would be any left in the barracks. But alas, armaments were another matter. When the last unit, a tank squad, passed by, we counted no more than thirteen tanks.

The festivities ended with a patriotic rally in the park, near the city hall. The principal speaker was the prime minister of Lithuania, who joyfully renamed Vilna the capital of his country. Then, obviously thinking of the Jewish refugees in the crowd, he added, "You can be sure that you will enjoy full freedom here with us."

The prime minister's words filled us with new hope, but on closer reflection we knew that the Russians had ulterior motives for presenting Vilna to the Lithuanians. The Lithuanians, poor lambs, were already in the mouth of the Russian bear, and Russia had only to choose an opportune moment to swallow them up.

During the weeks that followed, Reb Aharon did everything in his power to find a way for our yeshivah to leave Vilna for a permanent home in the free world. His father-in-law, Reb Isser Zalman Meltzer, wanted to have the yeshivah move to Jerusalem, where he himself had been living since 1925. *"Lomo atem yoshvim al har goesh ka-zeh?"* [Why do you remain sitting on top of a volcano?] he cabled to Reb Aharon, in Hebrew to elude the censors.

But the British would not let us into Palestine, no other country wanted us, and it seemed that we might have to remain in Lithuania for months, if not years. Reb Aharon decided that the yeshivah should move to a smaller place, deeper in Lithuania. In this way the students would be able to devote all their time to their studies, without the distractions and temptations of life in a big city.

Reb Aharon's choice fell on Yanova, a small town on the highway between Kovno and Riga. One day in February, 1940, we loaded our belongings onto rented trucks, climbed on top of our bundles and drove out of Vilna. Less than three hours later, we arrived in Yanova.

Yanova:
February — August, 1940

AS WE DROVE into Yanova, it seemed to us as if the town's whole Jewish population had turned out on the main street in our honor. We were escorted to the courtyard of the big synagogue for an official welcome. Rav Ginsburg, the rabbi of the town and a noted Talmudic scholar, delivered a welcoming address; so did the president of the Jewish community. Reb Aharon made a brief response. Afterwards, we were taken to the living quarters that had been prepared for us.

Life in Yanova was, indeed, very quiet, just as Reb Aharon had hoped. There was nothing to distract us from our studies. But Reb Aharon continued to search for a way of getting our yeshivah out of Europe, and some students made periodic trips to Kovno and Vilna in quest of opportunities to emigrate.

One day, much to my surprise and delight, I received a letter from Reb Gedalia Schorr in New York. During the months he had spent in Kletzk, he and I had become very good friends. Now he was anxious to help me. Enclosed in his letter was an affidavit signed by Reb Aaron Ziv, a leader of the American Agudath Israel youth movement. The affidavit was a guarantee to the American

Rabbi Gedalia Schorr זצ״ל,
Rosh Yeshivah,
Yeshivah Torah Vodaath
and Beth Medrash Elyon,
Monsey, NY

consular authorities that if they were to give me an American immigration visa and I settled in the United States, the American Agudah would help make certain that I did not become a public charge.

I considered myself already as good as in New York, because I had been born in Slutzk, which was part of the Soviet Union, and there were virtually no applicants on the Russian immigration quota for American visas. But my hopes were dashed when I found that my Russian birth certificate, which had been sent to me from Slutzk after endless wrangling with bureaucratic red tape, had somehow disappeared in the confusion of the past months. So I was no longer a privileged character and had to wait like everyone else for my turn to leave Lithuania.

We spent Purim and Passover of 1940 in Yanova, supported and cheered by the Jews of the town. Things seemed to be going as well for us as possible under the circumstances. Then, one morning early in June, 1940, the newspapers carried a report from the Soviet government press agency that a Russian soldier had been shot near the Lithuanian frontier by Lithuanian border police. Why did Stalin's propaganda machine give such prominence to so trivial an incident? The answer was obvious: the Soviets would use this occurrence — if, indeed, it had taken place at all — as a pretext for putting an end to Lithuania's independence.

ON SUNDAY, JUNE 5, 1940, Soviet tanks rolled into Lithuania. The Soviets took over with the usual explanation that they were doing so on the invitation of the masses. The takeover had been carefully planned; the Russians seemed to know every street and building in the territories they were

The End of Lithuanian Independence

A group of yeshivah students in Yanova, 1940.
Lower row, l. to r.: Alter Pekier, Yaakov Feinberg הי״ד, Mordechai Wenger ז״ל.
Upper row, l. to r.: Berl Pekier ז״ל, Herzl Greenberg הי״ד, David Melamed הי״ד

occupying. One day, in the street, I saw a Russian tank chugging back and forth over the same area again and again. The driver seemed to have lost his way. Finally, the tank stopped, and the driver asked me the way to the town of Vilkomir, not far from Yanova. When I gave him the directions, he took out a map, pointed to a spot on it, and said, "There should be a factory here." He was right. I told him that the factory had indeed once been there but had moved to another location. The Russian thanked me, climbed back into his tank and drove off.

The day in July, 1940, when Russia completed the annexation of Lithuania was a day of mourning for all the Jews, but particularly for us yeshivah students. Though we had long feared the possibility of a Communist invasion, we had not expected it to happen for at least another two years. By that time, we had hoped, we would be far away. But now, after barely nine months Lithuania became a Soviet republic. We who had fled from Kletzk with our yeshivah feared Soviet retribution and were filled with anxiety.

Desperate though we were, we missed at least one opportunity to save ourselves. We heard that the Japanese consul in Vilna was issuing immigration visas to Japan for two *lits* per person — the equivalent of fifty cents in those days. But most of the Jewish refugees, including the majority of the yeshivah students, did not act. The nominal fee made then suspicious. How could they know that the visas were genuine? And even assuming that the Japanese would honor the visas, the Russians surely would not permit us to leave. In fact, many of us suspected a Soviet trap; the Soviet secret police would take pictures of the applicants waiting on line in front of the Japanese consulate, accuse them of disloyalty to the Soviet Union and deport them to Siberia. Others, however, argued that Japan was a responsible nation with a decent government and would hardly permit its consular officials to offer fake visas for sale. Besides, the Russians might really allow the holders of Japanese visas to leave. In any event, anything was better than to vegetate in Lithuania under Communist rule. As a consequence, a large number of refugees, including most of the students of the Mirrer Yeshivah, went to

Vilna to apply for the visas and spent the war years in the comparative tranquility of China and Japan.

ON AUGUST 9, 1940, we received tragic news from Vilna. Rabbi Chaim Ozer Grodzensky had passed away. Although we knew that Reb Chaim Ozer had been in his late seventies, we yeshivah students felt uniquely bereft. He had been not only one of the greatest Torah scholars of our generation but also a most respected leader of organized Orthodox Jewry. It was to him, that all of us, including our own Rosh Yeshivah, Reb Aharon Kotler, had looked for guidance. Before the war, Reb Chaim Ozer received letters and visits from Jews all over the world, seeking his advice on personal and communal problems. One anecdote had it that a letter from distant Johannesburg, South Africa, addressed simply to "Rabbin Ch.O. Grodzenski, Zavalna 17," with the city and country

The Departure of Reb Chaim Ozer

Rabbi Chaim Ozer Grodzensky זצ״ל

omitted, had reached his home without undue delay. Many Jews traveled great distances to pay their respects to him and everyone, rich or poor, Sephardi or Ashkenazi, *chassid* or rationalist, received the same warm welcome at his humble apartment.

Far from our homes and loved ones, we yeshivah *bachurim* mourned Reb Chaim Ozer's death as our personal tragedy. We had loved and revered him as a father. A few words, or a blessing from him, had been enough to brighten our spirits for days. It was as if G-d Himself had sent Reb Chaim Ozer into our midst to soothe our aching hearts and to help replace the fathers and grandfathers we had left behind in our hometowns. And now he had departed from our midst, leaving us desolate.

Then we remembered the words of the prophet Isaiah, "Mipnei horo'eh ne'esaf hatzaddik" (the righteous are taken away just before calamity strikes). G-d snatches a tzaddik from this world, so as to spare him from suffering. Who knows, we said to each other, what trials were yet in store for us. We were more frightened when we remembered that the Torah world had lost another great soul, when the great Gaon Reb Boruch Lebovitz, of blessed memory, Rosh Yeshivah of Kamenetz, left this world just eight months before. These tragic passings so close to each other seemed ominous and we were full of foreboding. Just ten months later the Holocaust started ...

Death had come to Reb Chaim Ozer on Friday, two hours before the beginning of the Sabbath. Because mourning is forbidden on Shabbos, we tried to honor the day of rest with the customary rejoicing and good cheer, but our hearts were not in it. As soon as the Sabbath was over, we rented three trucks and, very early the next morning, led by Reb Aharon Kotler and Rabbi Ginsburg, we left Yanova for Vilna to attend the funeral.

THOSE OF US who made the journey to Vilna that day can never forget the scenes we passed as we approached Reb Chaim Ozer's

Reb Chaim Ozer's Funeral

home on Zavalna Street. Young and old, worldly merchants and simple working men, rabbis, yeshivah students and roshei yeshivah stood elbow to elbow, weeping bitterly.

Rabbi Boruch Ber Lebovitz and Rabbi Aharon Kotler, צז״ל

Some cried out, "Why have you left us now?" Along with thousands of others, we, the *bachurim* of Kletzk, stood in line, waiting to enter the apartment where Reb Chaim Ozer's body rested. Inside, we recited a few verses from the Psalms, then went out again to make room for others. Virtually all the Orthodox rabbis in Vilna had come to eulogize Reb Chaim Ozer. One of the first to speak was Reb Henoch Eiges of Vilna, author of the halachic work *Marcheshes*. His voice was so choked by sobs that we could not understand a word he was saying and could only weep with him. Afterwards, the cortege moved slowly through Trucka Street into German Street, to the courtyard of the synagogue, where additional eulogies were delivered by Reb Aaron Bakst, the Rav of Chavel; Reb Chizkiyah Yosef Mishkowski, the Rav of Krinki, Poland, who later settled in Israel, and Reb Moshe Shatzkes, the Lomzer Rav, who after the war became a highly respected rosh yeshivah at Yeshiva University in New York.

From the synagogue, the great mass of people that followed the coffin continued to the cemetery. The route to the cemetery led through a very narrow street. There, to our surprise, we saw young boys and girls wearing the red arm-bands of the Communist youth movement keeping order and directing the traffic. Had it not been for those young people, many of the mourners might have been trampled. It was rumored that even the Soviet bigwigs in Vilna had respected Reb Chaim Ozer, because they knew that he had sent food and other assistance to Communist sympathizers imprisoned in Fascist Poland before the war.

The eulogies at the graveside continued until well into the night. After the grave had been closed, we sadly returned to Yanova to prepare for yet another day of sorrow; the Fast of Tisha B'Av, two days later when our grief for Reb Chaim Ozer merged with our mourning for the fall of Jerusalem and the destruction of the Temple.

Reb Aharon Leaves

IT DID NOT TAKE LONG for the Soviet authorities to crack down on the yeshivos in Lithuania. The Russians did not want too many yeshivah students concentrated in one place, lest we infect others with our "obscurantist" views and set off a revolution against Stalin. One day we were informed that our own yeshivah, whose enrollment had grown from 200 to 250, would be permitted to continue only if we would disperse into three divisions, each settling in another place far from the centers of population.

And so we had to take leave of Yanova and the splendid Jews there, who had become our second fathers and mothers. As we loaded our bundles onto the trucks that were to take us away, these wonderful people wept, not only for us but also for themselves. What could Jews, and "bourgeois" ones at that, expect from the new Communist regime?

The students of our yeshivah were resettled in three villages near the Latvian border. One group, led by Reb Aharon himself, went to Salock, a village near the Latvian city of Dvinsk. Another group, under the care of the *mashgiach* (dean of students), Reb Yosef Leib Nenedick, moved to Dushat (now Dusheti, USSR), ten miles west of Salock. A third group, a select number of older advanced students, established themselves in Dukst, a little town that had once been part of Poland.

Rabbi Yosef Leib Nenedick
זצ"ל

My brother Berl and I were in the Salock contingent. We arrived in Salock late in August, 1940. The village consisted of a market place and four little streets. The Jews welcomed us warmly and helped us settle down in their own small Beth HaMedrash, where we promptly resumed our studies.

THE *YOMIM NORAIM* of 1940, the second High Holiday season of the war, found us even sadder and more insecure than the holidays of the previous year, when we still had been at home, in Kletzk. On Rosh HaShanah and Yom Kippur we wept as we entreated G-d, Who had saved us from the Nazis, to save us from the Communists also. Yet, *Neilah*, the closing service of Yom Kippur, left us so greatly cheered and comforted that we danced for sheer joy, certain that G-d had inscribed and sealed our names in His book of life and peace. We hoped that we would not have to stay in Salock for long but would soon receive visas to a better country, and that the

Life in Salock

46 / FROM KLETZK TO SIBERIA

Soviet authorities would then let us go. We were mentally and emotionally prepared to pull up stakes any day, but only for a journey to freedom, not for a trek even deeper into Soviet Russia.

It was incredibly difficult to travel anywhere from Salock, which was known as the "Siberia of Lithuania" because of its isolation. To get to Kovno one first had to travel six miles by horse and wagon, or on foot, to reach the nearest highway, and catch a bus for Kovno. To get to Vilna, it was a nine-mile trip, also by wagon or on foot, to reach the railroad station in Dukst, from where it was a full-night's train journey to Vilna. Nevertheless, we continued our trips to Kovno and Vilna in search of entry visas and exit permits.

Shortly after Sukkos the Soviet authorities announced that all those who had obtained immigration visas to other countries would be granted exit permits. We now realized that by failing to acquire the Japanese visas offered to us for two *lits*, we had lost our chance for freedom. Those who had bought the Japanese visas — including most of the Mirrer yeshivah community — immediately made arrangements to leave. Money was no problem. Jews who had to remain behind were glad to give the travelers whatever cash they possessed. Of what use, they said, would the money be to them in Communist Lithuania? They told the students that their credit was good. Once we are all out of here, they said, there will be time enough for us to get our money back.

Among the first scholars to leave was Reb Aharon's son, Reb Shneur Kotler. He had been lucky enough to obtain an immigration certificate for Palestine, and he eventually arrived in Eretz Yisrael by way of Turkey. Most of the others who left us during that period headed for Kobe, in Japan. Many of them went on from there to the United States.

ONE EVENING my brother Berl and I had a telephone call from Vilna. It was our sister Rochel. "Mother's here with me," she told us. "She heard rumors that you might be leaving, so she wants to see you and Berl before you go."

Mother Visits us

Berl and I took the evening train from Salock

REB AHARON LEAVES / 47

that very night and arrived in Vilna the next morning. We spent hours talking with our wonderful mother about life under the Russians in Kletzk and in Salock. We also took her to Kovno-Slobodka to visit her dear friend, Rebbetzin Kotler. The next few days passed all too quickly. Mother did not want to leave the family alone too long in Kletzk. Berl, Rochel and I wept as we saw her off at the station. It was the last time the four of us were to be together.

Meanwhile in Salock, Reb Aharon learned that Jewish leaders in the United States were sparing no efforts to get American immigration visas for him, the Rebbetzin and their daughter. Reb Aharon had visited the United States in 1935 and had met many influential Orthodox American Jews. Now he made contact with them, by cable and by telephone (using veiled language, of course), begging them to procure American visas also for the students of his yeshivah, because he did not want to leave as long as his *bachurim* were not safe. But his friends, both in Lithuania and New York, explained to him that by the time the students' visas came through — if, indeed, they would materialize within the foreseeable future — the Russians might have stopped issuing exit permits. But if Reb Aharon was in America, his personal influence might expedite the visas for his students so they could leave Lithuania before it was too late.

At first, Reb Aharon would not hear of leaving his boys, but shortly after the holidays something happened that helped change his mind. One Friday not long after Sukkos, while Reb Berl Starobin, the secretary of the yeshivah, was typing Reb Aharon's Talmudic commentaries on the yeshivah's battered Hebrew typewriter, three NKVD agents burst into the office, seized the typewriter and the papers, and ordered Reb Aharon to report to NKVD headquarters at seven o'clock that evening for interrogation. We, his students, were terrified but Reb Aharon did not betray any fear. After reciting the Friday evening *Kiddush* and finishing his Shabbos meal, he set out for NKVD headquarters alone. He would not allow anyone from the yeshivah to accompany him, because he did not want his interrogators to suspect how important he was to his students.

Reb Aharon Leaves

IT DID NOT TAKE LONG for the Soviet authorities to crack down on the yeshivos in Lithuania. The Russians did not want too many yeshivah students concentrated in one place, lest we infect others with our "obscurantist" views and set off a revolution against Stalin. One day we were informed that our own yeshivah, whose enrollment had grown from 200 to 250, would be permitted to continue only if we would disperse into three divisions, each settling in another place far from the centers of population.

And so we had to take leave of Yanova and the splendid Jews there, who had become our second fathers and mothers. As we loaded our bundles onto the trucks that were to take us away, these wonderful people wept, not only for us but also for themselves. What could Jews, and "bourgeois" ones at that, expect from the new Communist regime?

The students of our yeshivah were resettled in three villages near the Latvian border. One group, led by Reb Aharon himself, went to Salock, a village near the Latvian city of Dvinsk. Another group, under the care of the *mashgiach* (dean of students), Reb Yosef Leib Nenedick, moved to Dushat (now Dusheti, USSR), ten miles west of Salock. A third group, a select number of older advanced students, established themselves in Dukst, a little town that had once been part of Poland.

Rabbi Yosef Leib Nenedick
זצ"ל

My brother Berl and I were in the Salock contingent. We arrived in Salock late in August, 1940. The village consisted of a market place and four little streets. The Jews welcomed us warmly and helped us settle down in their own small Beth HaMedrash, where we promptly resumed our studies.

THE *YOMIM NORAIM* of 1940, the second High Holiday season of the war, found us even sadder and more insecure than the holidays of the previous year, when we still had been at home, in Kletzk. On Rosh HaShanah and Yom Kippur we wept as we entreated G-d, Who had saved us from the Nazis, to save us from the Communists also. Yet, *Neilah*, the closing service of Yom Kippur, left us so greatly cheered and comforted that we danced for sheer joy, certain that G-d had inscribed and sealed our names in His book of life and peace. We hoped that we would not have to stay in Salock for long but would soon receive visas to a better country, and that the

Life in Salock

Reb Aharon in NKVD Office

WHEN REB AHARON ARRIVED at NKVD headquarters, he was ordered to sit down at a table around which several NKVD officials were already seated. One of the Russians held up a sheet of paper with Hebrew typing on it. The agents had removed it from Reb Berl Starobin's typewriter.

"What's written on that paper?" the NKVD man wanted to know.

"Commentaries on the Talmud," Reb Aharon replied in the best Russian he could muster.

"Explain the subject matter in these commentaries," another NKVD man commanded.

"This happens to be a discourse on the relationship between Jewish servants and masters according to Jewish law," Reb Aharon answered, and proceeded to explain the intricacies of his discourse in Russian, a language he had not used in over twenty years.

One of the agents gave him a patronizing smile. "No one is really interested in your learned writings now. They are of no use to anyone."

"I cannot allow you to ridicule my religious beliefs," the Rosh Yeshivah replied in a quiet but self-assured voice. "They are sacred to me and Stalin has clearly stated in your Russian constitution that everyone is entitled to freedom of religion."

The NKVD man changed his strategy.

"Who are all the boys and young men with you in Salock?" one of the officials asked.

"I don't know," Reb Aharon replied. "They are not with me at present."

"How do they make a living?"

"I don't know."

"Aren't they rabbinical students?"

"I don't know. Maybe they are."

"We'll soon have elections for representatives to the Supreme Soviet. Will you vote?"

"Yes, I will vote," said Reb Aharon.

"For whom will you vote?"

"As the government will advise," Reb Aharon answered. Of course, in Soviet Russia there was only one party for which to vote.

After Reb Aharon's last reply the NKVD officials told him that he could go home.

"I'm back, *boruch Hashem!*" he said as he walked into his living quarters. Though all of us were greatly relieved that the Rosh Yeshivah had escaped from the lions' den unscathed, we realized that he was now in danger and that it was vital that he leave for America as soon as possible.

The story went at the time that in order to come to a decision, Reb Aharon resorted to a traditional device known as a *goral*. He took a *Chumash*, opened it and read the first passage that struck his eyes. The passage turned out to be the twenty-sixth verse of the sixth chapter in the Book of Exodus: "These are the Aaron and Moses to whom G-d said: Bring out the Children of Israel from the land of Egypt according to their hosts." Since his own name was Aaron, the Rosh Yeshivah understood that this meant that he must go forth from Russia and proceed to America, in order to help rescue all his students. As it turned out, Reb Aharon was one of the last to be able to leave Russia, for shortly afterwards the Soviet authorities stopped issuing exit permits.

Not only his own students but also many other Jews escorted Reb Aharon from Salock to the railroad station in Vilna. Many rabbis and other Jewish leaders from various Lithuanian cities, having heard of his imminent departure, likewise came to Vilna to take leave of Reb Aharon. We, his students, wept bitterly at parting from our teacher. Though we knew that once Reb Aharon was in America our own chances of being able to leave would improve, we felt lost and forsaken. Seventeen months earlier, we had left our parents and families; now we were to lose our spiritual father as well.

Returning to Salock, we felt very depressed. The yeshivah group that had moved to Dushat still had their *mashgiach*, Reb Yosef Leib Nenedick, but we in Salock had no one left to inspire us. Only the sacred words of the Torah were still there to keep up our spirits. We sought comfort in the Talmudic tractate we

A group of yeshivah students in Salock, 1941.

happened to be studying at the the time — I recall it was Tractate Betza — and we realized how much truth there was in the words of Psalm 19: "The precepts of the L-rd are upright, rejoicing the heart."

The Yeshivah Breaks Camp

DURING THE WINTER OF 1940-41 our spirits lifted a little. We knew that the Rosh Yeshivah, Reb Aharon, arrived safely in New York. We felt certain that we would soon receive immigrant visas for the United States or some other safe country. We were right, for shortly after Reb Aharon's arrival in the United States, we received visas for the South American republic of Chile. It was clear to us that this was the work of Reb Aharon. We were afire with excitement at the prospect of leaving the Lithuanian SSR. Unfortunately, our rejoicing was premature, for we were informed that the Soviet authorities had stopped issuing exit permits. Had we received our Chilean visas one month earlier, we would have been free. However, it seemed to be the will of G-d that we remain under the Soviet yoke for a little longer.

When we first learned that our Chilean visas would be of no use to us, our spirits plummeted from optimism to despair. Many of the students whose hometowns, like our own Kletzk, had been occupied by Soviet forces, considered leaving the yeshivah community and returning to their families. Such moves entailed considerable difficulty, since our yeshivah community was in the Lithuanian SSR while our hometowns, for the most part, now belonged to another Soviet republic, that of White Russia. Still, the red tape would not have been insuperable except for the fact that most of us *bachurim* felt that, in the present uncertain situation, the yeshivah students should remain together.

Once again, our studies saved us from giving way to

despondency. We knew that, in the words of Jeremiah, *"es tzarah he leYaakov"* (a time of distress had come for Jacob), but we prayed that the second part of that verse, *"umimenah yivoshea"* (but he will be saved from it), would apply also in our case, for we were aware that, as the Talmud tells us, salvation could come from heaven in the twinkling of an eye.

On Purim, 1941, we tried our best to enter into the spirit of exuberant rejoicing proper for that holiday, and as we bellowed our contempt every time the name of evil Haman was read from the Megillah, we thought of the Communist Hamans as well and fervently hoped that they would meet the same end as the wicked prime minister of ancient Persia.

Four weeks later, we celebrated Passover. The rabbi of Salock, a scholar and a most devout individual, his wife, and the other Jews of the town did their best to make it a happy season for us, complete with the required Passover foods.

Spring had come again, full of beauty and promise, but our hearts were filled with sadness. We were certain that the Soviets would not permit our yeshivah to exist very much longer. They would break up our yeshivah, and what would happen to us then? It seemed that we could do nothing but wait for the Soviets to make the next move. With every passing day, we felt more and more helpless and frustrated.

EARLY IN MAY, 1941, we, the yeshivah students, received a summons from the *starosta* (county chief) of our district to go to

We are Summoned to Zarasai

Zarasai, our county seat, to register at the *rayonspolkome* (county office) there. So we hired several horses and wagons and set out for Zarasai. Talking on the way, we decided that the summons from the *starosta* could mean only one thing: our legal status was about to be clarified.

Our first stop in Zarasai was at the home of the town's rabbi, who was both learned and kind. He calmed us down with gentle words of reassurance. With G-d's help, he said, all would yet be well.

At the *starosta's* office we were handed some forms to

complete. We were asked to fill in our dates and places of birth and to state whether we wished to remain in Russian territory or to leave; if the latter, we had to name the country to which we hoped to emigrate. We considered our answers very carefully, fearful that our fate might well depend on our replies. All of us gave the same reply: we declared that we wished to emigrate to the United States, or to Palestine, or to Chile (in view of our Chilean visas). After handing in our forms, we were told to go home. Not a word was said about our future. We returned to Salock that same evening, not knowing whether to be relieved or disappointed.

We spent the weeks that followed — including the holiday of Shavuos — in a mood alternating between high hopes and vague apprehension. On Friday, June 6, 1941, we received another official summons for registration, this time with the *selkom* or village sheriff's office. At the *selkom* we were asked only one question: Did we wish to remain under Russian sovereignty and to apply for Soviet citizenship? We were given three hours to decide whether our answer was "yes" or "no." Once again, we felt our answer would seal our fate.

We remembered that one year earlier, in 1940, the Jews of Bialystok and the surrounding area had been asked to make a similar choice. After Germany and the Soviet Union carved up Poland between themselves, thousands of Jews who had fled to Bialystok from central Poland to escape the Germans found themselves in Russian territory. Eventually, the Soviet authorities asked them whether they wished to remain in the city permanently and accept Soviet citizenship or to return to their hometowns, which were now occupied by Germany. Strange to relate, a number of these Jews opted to return to their original homes. They were so fed up with life under Communism that they could not imagine anything worse, not even under German occupation. Who could have surmised Hitler's ultimate plans for the Jews? In any event, the Jews in Bialystok who had stated their preference for the Germans over the Russians never reached their hometowns. As a punishment for spurning Soviet citizenship, the Russian authorities deported them to Siberia.

Knowing what had happened in Bialystok, we yeshivah *bachurim* found it difficult to make a decision. Many in our group believed it would be better to opt for Soviet citizenship than to have to struggle for survival in the Siberian wilderness. Others, however, felt that we should frankly state our desire to leave Europe. Perhaps the Soviet authorities would eventually reconsider their stand and give us exit permits. Accepting Soviet citizenship, on the other hand, seemed to us an irrevocable step and might mean a lifetime under Communist oppression, particularly since we, as yeshivah students, had incurred the suspicion and hatred of the Soviets because of our religious convictions.

Moments of Decision

FOR THE NEXT three hours we weighed the advantages and disadvantages of accepting the Soviet offer. Shaul Goldman (or Shaul Lutzker, as we called him because he came from Lutzk), now a rosh yeshivah in Brooklyn, New York, was the first to announce his decision. He declared that he would never become a Soviet citizen. He knew that his refusal might send him to Siberia, but then all of Russia was one big prison. I agreed with Shaul, and the rest of the group followed our lead, except for Moshe Zigman, of Brest-Litovsk, and Yaakov Feinberg, of Kletzk. Moshe and Yaakov chose to become Soviet citizens because they feared they would never be able to survive the hardships of Siberia; besides, they hoped to return to their hometowns, which were now also under Russian occupation.

We went home and prepared for Shabbos. Our sister had come from Vilna to visit us. She had married our good friend Mordechai Wenger in a civil ceremony so that she could go to the United States whenever Berl and I were ready to leave.

Friday evening, June 13, we *davened*, ate our Shabbos meal and sang *z'miros*, unaware of the fate that awaited us.

Early the next morning, we were awakened by an insistent knock on the door of the building in which we were quartered. We saw a gang of young Jewish Communists outside: later, we learned that they had been hand-picked by the local Soviet authorities to "process" us. They told us that we were to report immediately to the *selkom*. Looking out the windows that opened on the market place, we saw large buses, the kind that were used for public transportation in Kovno and other large cities. The Communist youths informed us that these buses would transport us from Salock to the train station of Dukst, on the first leg of our journey to Siberia.

Our first impulse was to attempt to escape into the woods not far from our building. My brother Berl and I got to the woods, but we soon realized that the sparse forest would not afford us much cover from the police. We would probably be caught and severely punished. And so after a while, we walked back to the village, through back alleys in order to avoid the market place and any police who might be looking for us.

WE STOPPED at the home of a fine Jewish family where I had often been invited for Shabbos meals. When they saw Berl and me,

Goodbye to Freedom

they burst into tears because they had already heard what was happening at our yeshivah. We hurriedly recited the *Kiddush* and washed our hands but found it difficult to swallow even the *ke-zayyis** of food mandatory for a Sabbath meal. Our wonderful hosts offered to find hiding places for us. But when we heard their eldest son whisper to his parents that anyone who would give us shelter would surely have trouble with the authorities, we decided to leave. We did not want to jeopardize the safety of these good people, who had always been so kind to my brother and me. Tearfully and with great reluctance, our hosts let us go.

Almost as soon as we reached the street, Berl and I were seized by a grim-faced policeman who, without uttering a word, took us to the police station.

At the police station we met most of the other yeshivah students. Some of them stood quietly, seemingly resigned to their fate, but several others sought to escape. One of them, a boy from Rakov, jumped from a window of the police station. Another, a

---

* Literally, a quantity the size of an olive, but actually nearer the volume of an egg. This is the minimum quantity of food required for a ritual meal.

native of Mush, also escaped and, as we later learned, hid out for a while in the attic of the village synagogue. Both boys escaped deportation to Siberia, but their "luck" proved to be their undoing when the Germans turned on the Russians, and Salock was occupied by German troops. Eventually, our two friends perished at the hands of the Nazis.

Most of us remained as calm as possible during the "processing" at the police station, but there were a few who could not control themselves. One of the boys shouted at the police officers, "What do you want from us? Is it a crime to say that I want to go to America?" The police did not react; they could hardly have cared less about the opinions of a Jewish theological student.

Berl and I wondered what had become of Rochel, who was staying with one of the local Jewish families. Would she, too, be deported to Siberia with us?

The Long Journey East

AFTER THE POLICE CLERKS had finished registering us, we were escorted by armed policemen to our homes to pick up clothing and bedding. On the street we passed Moshe Zigman. Now it was quite clear to us: Those who had rejected Soviet citizenship were about to be deported, while those who, like Moshe, had opted to become citizens of the Soviet Union remained free. Moshe stopped in his tracks and mouthed to me, in Yiddish, the words, "I pray I'll never have reason to envy you." Alas, his words turned out to be more prophetic than he knew.

By the time we had gathered our belongings and had boarded the buses, the sun had set. A crowd of local Jews watched us leave, and we spotted Rochel in the crowd. Our friends tossed food through the windows of our buses but we were not allowed to thank them. I will never forget our last sight of them, and of our sister Rochel, weeping as they shouted their farewells to us.

Though Rochel was among those who had refused Soviet citizenship, the police in Salock took no interest in her because she was under jurisdiction of the authorities in Vilna. As we learned much later, she decided not to stay in Vilna but to return to Kletzk, because she did not want to leave our parents there alone. That was how she and our parents shared the fate of the 4,500 Jews who were murdered by the Nazis in Kletzk on October 30, 1941 (9 Cheshvan, 5702).

We, the yeshivah students, were not the only ones to be deported to Siberia that day in June. Many native Lithuanians, both Jews and gentiles, who were considered suspect by the Soviet, were dragged from their homes and herded into the buses together with us. We talked to a Lithuanian woman, who had been seized with her two young children in place of her husband, a former employe of the Lithuanian government who had taken off for parts unknown. Later, we learned that Aleksandras Stulginskis, a former president of the Lithuanian republic, had also been deported to Siberia.

THERE WERE STARS in the sky and Shabbos was over by the time our buses deposited us at the train station of Dukst. A long

Locked In a Boxcar

train of boxcars was waiting for us there. We were divided into groups of thirty-five; one group for each boxcar. Berl and I looked around the boxcar that was to be our home — we did not suspect it then — for more than three weeks. The car was sealed from the outside to prevent the passengers from escaping. On either side of our car there were two openings with grates across them; there were two long tiers of boards; these were our bunks for sleeping. Our sanitary facilities consisted of one hole in the floor of our car. At first we were mortified, but eventually we became accustomed to this lack of privacy.

Too exhausted to unpack, we spent our first night on the train without much sleep. The train remained in the station all that night. The next morning we still had not moved. The word spread that the police was still searching for people on their deportation list who apparently had gone into hiding.

We began to settle down our bundles and sleep. More wagons were added to our train to accommodate deportees from other localities in the Zarasai district.

At last, on Tuesday morning, June 17, we began to move. Our first stop, two hours later, was Swencany, near Vilna, where our train took on three more cars, packed with deportees from other parts of Lithuania. Our next stop was Vileyka, the last station near the former Russian-Polish border. We remained there until Saturday morning.

Most of the passengers in our boxcar were yeshivah students, but there were also a few gentiles, including a professor who had taught at the high school in Chavel and a wealthy Lithuanian farmer and his wife. Each morning, we Jews held a *shacharis* service. Our gentile fellow passengers watched us with great respect, and some of them wept.

On Saturday, June 21, one week after we boarded the buses in Salock our train pulled out of Vileyka and half an hour later we entered Russia proper. Standing on the boards that served as our bunks, and craning our necks, we looked through the tiny windows of our boxcar and got our first view of the Russian countryside. We could see the difference between the peasants of Poland and Lithuania and those of Russia. The Russian peasants were dressed in rags, wearing slippers instead of shoes, and in every village through which we passed, we could see long lines in front of the country stores.

I remembered seeing Russian peasants coming to Kletzk to shop for food and clothing that they said they could not get at home. But only now, seeing for myself the places where these unfortunates lived, could I understand how downtrodden the people of the Russian countryside really were. I recalled that one day, back in Kletzk, a Russian *politruk* (political commissar) had

THE LONG JOURNEY EAST / 59

stood up in the market place and assured whoever would listen that the Russian people lacked for nothing under the Communist system. Someone from the audience had shouted, "And do you also have oranges in Russia?" the *politruk*, caught off-balance, unthinkingly replied, "*Kanietchno, wminsku veliki zavod yest* (Certainly, there's a big orange factory in Minsk)."

Now, looking out from our boxcar windows, we saw the meager produce of the Soviet fields, the stubby ears of corn and the barren, rocky soil, and we could see with our own eyes how the people of Russia had been misled and deceived by their Communist overlords.

Deep in Soviet Russia

BY THE TIME our train pulled into Minsk — the city of the alleged "orange factory" — we had become accustomed, or perhaps resigned, to boxcar conditions. Every other day our car was briefly unlocked by NKVD men who distributed loaves of bread, one loaf for every two individuals, and buckets of hot and cold water. Occasionally, there were bowls of soup with tiny pieces of meat swimming in the thin broth. Of course, we did not touch the soup, but thanks to the food we still had left from the farewell gifts our good Jews in Salock had thrown to us, we did not go hungry. We spent most of our days praying; there was nothing else for us to do.

One evening, as we were singing yeshivah melodies in an attempt to forget our troubles for a while, the door of our boxcar opened and several NKVD officers, their rifles ready to shoot, burst into the car. We stopped singing at once.

"*Zdies ravini yest?* (Any rabbis in here?)" one of the officers demanded.

"*Nyet*," we replied.

"*Slichali modlitra?* (Then what are those prayers you've been chanting?)"

When we said that we had been singing songs, not prayers, the Russians shouted at us: "Don't start singing again. Nobody wants to hear your songs."

Needless to say, we did not dare to sing again for the rest of our journey.

As the days went by, we, the yeshivah students, began to talk with the Lithuanian gentiles who shared our plight. They told us about their former lives, and we spoke of the years we had spent in Kletzk, studying at our yeshivah. The Lithuanians admired us for our faith and optimism, but in fact we were often very depressed, especially when we thought of our homes and families that we had left behind.

During our layover in Minsk the men were separated from the women and children, who were put into other cars. There were heart-rending wails as families were torn apart. The Lithuanians were beginning to understand how we Jews felt, wondering whether we would ever see our families again.

On Monday afternoon, June 23, we left Minsk. Bypassing the well-known cities of Borisov, Orsha and Bobroysk, we arrived in Smolensk. There we first heard that Germany had invaded Russia. A policeman who was standing guard entered our car and unhappily told us that the Russians were losing one city after the other, that Western Belorussia, including the city of Baranovice, was already in German hands and that German troops were approaching Minsk.

We slept well that night, hoping somewhat naively that, if the Germans were really close by, we might be able to take advantage of the confusion and escape. Somehow, in our bewilderment, we did not stop to consider that it would be better for us to remain prisoners of the Russians that to be captured by Hitler's troops.

After a few hours in Smolensk we continued our journey eastward. Our train no longer stopped at passenger stations but only at freight terminals so that, for several days, we did not know what places we were passing. Only from the direction of the sunrise could we conclude that we were traveling due east.

ONE DAY OUR TRAIN stopped at Saratov, a large city near the Volga river. There, for the first time in weeks, we were allowed

In the Ural Mountains

off the train long enough to be taken to a public bathhouse. Though we were pale from weeks without sun and air, we emerged from the public showers refreshed and invigorated from our brief taste of freedom. We were allowed altogether three hours to enjoy the heavenly outdoor air before we were herded back into the boxcars.

Locked up in our boxcars, we traveled on for many days until we reached Ufa, a large city in the Ural Mountains. We were now in Asiatic Russia. We were ordered to leave our car with our belongings so that we could be counted. The guard was changing, and our departing jailers had to hand over to our new "escorts" the exact amount of human "merchandise" they had received. After we had been counted and duly re-registered, we were transferred to another train.

The Soviet officials who were to escort us the rest of the way gave us bread, soup and cold water. We knew that we were traveling deeper into Asia but were not sure whether we were really going to Siberia or heading for camps in a warmer, healthier region. Once again, we turned to the sun for guidance. If the sun showed that the train was still going due east, we would know that we were on our way to Siberia, but if we were going south, our destination was probably Kazakhstan. Anything, we thought, would be better than Siberia.

The sun indicated that we were still moving east; so we understood that we were bound for Siberia. We prayed to G-d to grant us the strength and stamina to withstand the cold and hardships of Siberian exile. Soon, the place names we passed confirmed our apprehensions: Omsk, Novosibirsk, Tomsk, Krasnoyarsk, and Reshoti. We were indeed in Siberia.

Labor Camp Number Seven: June — October, 1941

ON MONDAY AFTERNOON, July 6, 1941, after twenty-three days in crowded, fetid boxcars, we arrived at our destination, a labor camp deep in a forest, on the road to Vladivostok, somewhere between Krasnoyarsk and Irkutsk, seven miles from Reshoti. Our camp was called Labor Camp Number Seven. This meant that six other camps of similar type had already been set up in the region.

The Siberian summer lasts only ten weeks, but during that time temperatures can soar to 130 degrees Fahrenheit. Fortunately, the weather was not humid, but in the torrid afternoon, when the sun was about to set, the mosquitoes turned up in thick swarms. When we left our train at about four o'clock on the day of our arrival, the air was already thick with mosquitoes. The frogs of the Ten Plagues could not have covered more of Egypt than the mosquitoes covered Siberia.

We were desperate. Could we ever survive this hell? we wondered. Were we truly such a menace to society that we deserved to be taken to this G-dforsaken place?

As we entered the camp, we were ordered to hand over our valuables to the guards. We were given receipts for rings and wrist watches, but our *talleisim, tefillin* and prayer books were confiscated outright.

We were then escorted to our barracks; I found myself in a cabin containing little more than its four walls. We were given bowls of thick noodle soup, luckily without meat. Starved as we were, the soup tasted good. If this was to be our daily fare, I thought, we might survive better than I had feared. Unfortunately, this turned out to be the only time we were to be served such a nourishing meal.

Our sleeping accommodations consisted of two rows of wide boards, one on top of the other, piled with sacks of straw. We used the blankets we had brought with us from home. Thirty-five men shared one tier of boards. We slept so closely packed together that whenever one of us turned on his side during the night, the others beside us had to turn also. Nevertheless, no one had trouble sleeping that first night.

The next day we were allowed to rest from our journey. We inspected our new home. The camp was a virtual prison, surrounded by a thick wall. A barbed-wire fence ran eight feet from the wall, inside the camp grounds. This fence, we were informed, was the border beyond which we were not permitted to move unescorted. On all four corners of the camp wall there were observation towers manned by soldiers with loaded rifles pointing down at us, the prisoners. These soldiers were under orders to shoot, without warning, anyone who took a step over the fence.

In the evening we were escorted into the camp bathhouse for a warm shower. Then we were shaved from head to toe by other inmates who had been barbers in their hometowns. Feeling refreshed and clean, we returned to our barracks to sleep. But the next morning, very early, we had a rude awakening. I could hardly recognize some of my bunkmates, because their faces were swollen beyond recognition. The mosquitoes had made their nightly rounds. The camp administration gave us gauze sheets to protect us from the mosquitoes during the evening hours, when the plague was always at its worst. But to my happy surprise I found that I never needed protection; the mosquitoes seemed to keep away from me, at least.

OUR FIRST DAY of work began at six o'clock that morning, with a shrill bell for reveille. We leaped from our bunks and washed. Each of us *davened shacharis* for himself because there was no time to gather for regular morning services. By six-thirty we were to report at the camp gate for our work assignments.

Siberian Hard Labor

At the gate we found hundreds of other inmates already waiting to be divided into "work brigades." Most of the inmates of Camp Number Seven were Lithuanians, non-Jewish businessmen and intellectuals. Later we learned that most of the students from yeshivos other than our own (except for the Mirrer community, which had already left for the Far East) had been taken to other camps. In Labor Camp Number Seven, aside from our own group of yeshivah students from Kletzk, there was only one other group of yeshivah *bachurim*, boys from the yeshivah of Radin. They were fortunate enough to have with them their Rosh Yeshivah, Reb Avrohom Tropp, who was to become head of the yeshivah of Stolin in Brooklyn, where he remained until his death.

Each "work brigade" was permitted to choose one of its own men to serve as "brigade commander," a kind of liaison officer between the inmates and the camp administration. The commander of our Kletzk brigade was Reb Yosef Nevenansky, who after the war was a rosh yeshivah in Yeshivah Rabbi Jacob Joseph in New York (he died in 1968). The commander of the Radin brigade was Reb Dovid Zaritzky, who became a well-known writer for Orthodox newspapers after the war (he recently died in Jerusalem).

After the brigade assignments had been completed, the camp commander, a major in the Red Army, gave us our orders. We were to complete a specified work quota each day; if we failed to do so, our food rations would be reduced. He also warned us that if this penalty would not be sufficient incentive to make us work harder, there would be more severe punishments. After this cheerful announcement, the major assigned one soldier, armed with a rifle, to take charge of each brigade. This soldier, we were informed, would escort us to our places of work, make certain

Rabbi Yosef Nevenansky זצ״ל   *Rabbi Dovid Zaritzky* זצ״ל

that we did not lounge about like capitalists with nothing to do, and in the evening, bring us back to the camp.

As we marched through the camp gate on our way to our work area, which was in the woods about five kilometers away, our soldier ordered us to walk four abreast, not too fast, and to keep in step. Anyone disobeying or attempting to escape would be shot immediately. He followed close behind us, his gun at the ready. He repeated his instructions and warnings every morning before we left the camp. We were permitted to talk with one another while we walked, as long as we kept our voices down.

WE NOTED THAT during the summer months the sun rose long before reveille time at six, so that morning prayers could be recited as early as five-thirty. This made it possible for us to organize a *minyan* for regular *shacharis* services in our bunk. Though our bodies cried out for that extra half hour of sleep, we yeshivah *bachurim* gladly got up half an hour earlier so we

Siberia Did Not Change Our Determination

could have our morning service and still be ready in time to report for work.

One morning, as we were *davening*, our prayers were interrupted by one of our barrack mates, a young man in his early twenties. He was weeping bitterly. "Why are you crying?" I asked him. "We're all in the same boat. We should have faith in the Almighty that He will save us soon."

"That's just it," the young man replied. "That's why I'm so despondent. I have no faith, no religion. I was born in Soviet Russia and raised as a Communist. I envy your faith in G-d, because it will help you survive this miserable existence and you will live to enjoy your freedom again, while I will surely die. I don't even know the reason why they sent me to this place, but I do know that I won't be able to stand it much longer."

And so he kept on crying while we continued our prayers.

When the days grew shorter so that it was still dark at five-thirty, we found another way of *davening* together each morning. We recited our prayers as we marched from the camp to our place of work, four abreast. One of the yeshivah men walking on the inside acted as *baal tefillah*, leading us in the prayers. But since loud talking was forbidden, not everyone could hear him, so that only those walking in the lines immediately ahead and in back of him could join in the responses.

The five-kilometer march from Labor Camp Number Seven to our place of work took us about an hour and a half. We marched most of the way on a bed of railroad tracks, but once we were inside the woods we walked on narrow paths that wound among the tall trees. The trunks of the trees were so thick that if two people placed their arms around one of the tree trunks from either side, their hands would not meet.

When we first arrived at our work site, we were given a lecture by a Russian engineer who told us our duties and our work objectives. The Soviet government, he explained, needed lumber to be processed quickly for export. For maximum speed and efficiency in transportation, the railroads had to pick up the lumber directly from its place of origin. Therefore the tracks had to be extended from the highway deeper and deeper into the woods. The tracks between which we had marched along the highway had been laid by prisoners like ourselves. Our work now was to add to them. But before we could lay the tracks, we had to uproot trees and drain the ground, which in spots was dangerously swampy.

We, the yeshivah boys, were stunned. Most of us had hardly ever knocked a nail into a wall, or indeed used our muscles for any activity much more strenuous than turning the folios of a *Gemara*. Now we were expected to perform work that demanded immense physical strength. We knew that we would never be able to do that without the help of G-d.

Our guard pointed to trees on four sides of a certain area. These trees, he said, marked the boundaries beyond which we would not be permitted to move. Anyone found working beyond that area without permission would be summarily shot. Anyone who needed to relieve himself had to ask the guard, "*Grazdanin strelock magu adpravlatza* (Mister Soldier, may I go and clean myself)?" The guard would then point to some trees further off in the woods to which the prisoner could go for privacy. However, he was warned to go no further. This was not an idle threat; one day an inmate, who had once been the postmaster of Salock and was a little deaf, unwittingly passed the arbitrary boundary by only a few meters. The guard shot him, crippling him for life.

We were given a daily quota of trees to uproot. Those who failed to meet that quota received only two-thirds of that day's food ration, which was actually a starvation diet. Because it was virtually impossible to uproot these huge, thick trees, we had to saw off the trunks as close to the roots as possible, and then pull out the remaining stump with the roots.

WE WERE DIVIDED into groups of four, one group to each tree, and began to work. The tree assigned to my group was in swampy ground. The four of us took off our shoes and found ourselves ankle-deep in mud. The Lithuanian gentiles, to whom tree-felling seemed to be child's play, worked much more quickly than we. But when our own gigantic tree came crashing

Always, with Hope to G-d

down, we felt really pleased with ourselves. Here was proof that we yeshivah *bachurim* were also willing and able to work hard. Pulling out the thick, heavy roots of our tree was more difficult. We had to dig through the earth until we exposed the entire system of roots; then we hacked each root into pieces to pull the whole tangle out.

From noon to one o'clock we had one hour's rest, during which we could do nothing but lie on the ground, exhausted. At one o'clock the bell rang, ordering us back to work. It always seemed to ring much too soon. At six in the evening, we were ordered to line up and marched, four abreast, back to our camp, the same way as we had come, with the same guard as our escort, with the rifle pointed straight at us. We arrived at the camp after seven o'clock, dead tired and ravenously hungry.

Our return to the camp was greeted each evening by an inmate orchestra playing lilting waltzes. After a while even I, who love all music, particularly waltzes, found the scraping of the violins grating on my nerves.

We went directly to the mess lines to pick up our day's rations. Those who had completed the day's work quota received a pound and a half of bread, and a bowl of noodle soup. Most of the time we yeshivah students could not complete our quota, so we got only one pound of bread and a thin soup of hot water with a few noodles floating in it. The loaves we received were much smaller and heavier than the fluffy loaves of bread sold at grocery stores in America. The camp baker, a real Asiatic Russian type, probably sold some of the flour he had been given, pocketed the money and made up for the missing flour by adding more water to the dough; this made our loaves of bread not only small and heavy but also very crumbly.

We clutched our bread rations tightly so as not to lose a single precious crumb. Many *bachurim* ate their whole ration at one time because they were starved, and they subsisted for the next twenty-four hours on the "soup." Others, including myself, divided our bread rations into three portions to be eaten at different times during the day, rather than stuff ourselves with food all at once. As a consequence, we were always hungry.

In those days we invented a new delicacy. We made a fire with whatever splinters of wood we could find, and boiled water into which we put small pieces of bread. The result was a bread soup which we starved creatures relished. "This is delicious!" we would say to each other, "Why didn't we ever make it at home?" We really meant it — at the time.

We did not always do the same work. At first, our job was to uproot trees. Later, we were ordered to saw lumber and move huge logs from one place to another. But no matter what our work, we yeshivah *bachurim* could never fill our daily quota. And so we never received our full food ration.

One day we were ordered to move firewood from one place to another. After having dragged heavy logs, we considered this a relatively easy task. We worked without a stop in hopes of finally filling our daily work quota and receiving a full day's ration. But our hopes were abruptly dashed when the inmate assigned to pile up the firewood, who was not exactly an engineer, miscalculated and the whole pile of wood came tumbling down. Miraculously, no one was injured, but all our hours of work had gone for nothing. We burst into tears, fearing that our guard would accuse us of sabotage, a crime punishable by death. Spent in both body and spirit, we started all over again and eventually managed to rebuild the pile of firewood. When our supervisor showed up, we tearfully explained to him why we had fallen behind in our work. Luckily, he was sympathetic and said nothing further. When we returned to the camp that evening, we were relieved to find that our food ration was, at least, no less than what we usually received. But the anxiety of the day depressed us for days thereafter.

OUR HUNGER was intense. Once, as we marched to work, we noticed a pile of potato peelings on the ground to the right of the tracks. Without giving a thought to what might happen if our armed escort saw us step out of line, we scooped up the dirty potato peelings and devoured them, risking our lives for refuse we would heedlessly throw into our garbage cans today. Fortunately

Hungry, but Not in Spirit

the guard seemed to understand and did not shoot at us, but we knew that we had taken a big chance. We remembered the Prophet Jeremiah's vivid characterization of the agony of hunger: *"Tovim hayo challelai cherev me-challelai ro-ov"* (those who died by the sword were better off than those who died of hunger).

One day the camp supervisor, apparently having received reports about our poor performance, came to the woods to watch the yeshivah students at work. He began to demonstrate to us how we could improve our output, but he soon stopped and left in disgust. When we returned to the camp that evening we did not get our food rations and were marched off to spend the night in the guardhouse.

The guardhouse was much worse than our barracks. We had to sleep on sacks without even a semblance of pillows and were given only bread, no soup.

We spent most of the night praying to G-d to give us the strength and courage to go on. When we awoke the next morning, most of us felt a little better. Truly, G-d gives strength to the weary. And so, when we were released from the guardhouse, we joined the other brigades for the daily roll call and set out for work.

At midnight on *motzoei* Shabbos — Saturday night, August 30, 1941 — two months after our arrival at the Labor Camp Number Seven, there was a pounding on our barracks door, and a group of camp officials marched in, holding sheets of paper. From these papers they read off a list of names, explaining that the prisoners whose names were read would be released at once. Among those released were our own brigade commander, Reb Yosef Nevenansky, Reb Leib Botkin (who later settled in Brooklyn) and Leib Altman (who was to die of starvation and illness somewhere in Russia). These men were ordered to pack their belongings and to report at the camp entrance as quickly as possible. Of course the rest of us were sad to be left behind, but we were happy for our friends, not least because their release gave us hope that before long we, too, might be freed.

Not until several weeks later did we learn why these friends had been released. They were Polish citizens who, under an agreement between Stalin and the Polish government-in-exile in London, were released from Soviet labor camps to help fight the common enemy: Nazi Germany. This agreement was observed in every Soviet labor camp. One young Polish Jew was released from a Soviet prison ship and eventually joined a division of the Polish liberation army that had been organized in Russia. His unit was assigned to the Middle East, and so he arrived in Palestine in May, 1942. His name was Menachem Begin.

We were too excited to sleep that night. But at daybreak Sunday morning, we started off, as usual, for our work site. It seemed to us that the Russians made us work harder than they usually did; apparently, they did not want us to get the idea that our release, too, was at hand.

Shabbos was just another working day for us. If we had refused to work on Saturdays for religious or any other reasons, it would have meant certain death for us. Under the circumstances there could be no question of our observing Shabbos by not working. But in order not to forget that it was Shabbos, we performed our tasks differently from our weekday style. For instance, one yeshivah *bachur* worked on Shabbos with his spade held in reverse position. But the guard saw him and pointed his gun at him. Immediately, the boy turned his spade to the correct position. The Russians would not tolerate any change, no matter how slight, in our routine.

ONE MORNING, a week before Rosh HaShanah, as we were about to leave for our work site, we were notified that our brigade could have one day off. We were surprised and happy, but also a little suspicious. At noon one of the camp administrators came to speak to us. He spoke calmly and deliberately, and each of his words cut into us like a knife. We were miserable exiles, he told us, and were here to work, not to rest and play. Those who worked hard and fulfilled their quota would survive. They would receive larger rations of food, perhaps even extra rations, and they would not find life too difficult. But those who failed to meet their work requirements would suffer. The purpose of our one day of freedom was to let

Wishful Thinking

us regain our strength. If we continued falling short of our daily quota, we would not survive for very long. The camp administrator refused to listen to our argument that, no matter how many days of rest we might be given, we were physically unable to work harder than we already did each day.

After the Russian official had left, one of the yeshivah *bachurim* broke down. "They want to keep us here forever!" he sobbed. "I think we're all going to die in Siberia!"

We could not think of an answer to comfort our friend.

Except for that one special day off, we were never again allowed a day of rest. We spent seven full days each week at hard labor. One Sunday we were notified that we should not go to our work site but remain in our barracks. But that day of enforced idleness left us more spent than a day of slave labor in the woods. We were told that all inmates would be searched to make sure than we were not concealing smuggled goods. We were ordered to gather our belongings, including our bedding, take them to a designated place near the camp gate and wait there until the search of our barrack, our belongings and our bodies had been completed.

After we had left our barracks, the camp officials went inside and searched every nook and cranny, each crack in the wall, for contraband. Then they came out to us, turned our meager bundles inside out and searched the pockets of all our clothes. We had to stand outdoors under the burning Siberian midsummer sun until our bundles had been checked. Those who were fortunate enough to be searched first were allowed to return to the barracks and rest. I, unfortunately, was one of the last to be checked and had to stand in the torrid sun until four o'clock that afternoon. When I was finally allowed to drag myself back to my quarters, I was hardly able to stand on my feet.

During that search the camp officials confiscated items that had been overlooked when we first arrived at Labor Camp Number Seven. The "contraband" included many *talleisim* and *tefillin* that had escaped the attention of the camp guards at the time of our arrival.

We did not know what other articles would be considered

"illegal." Two students of the yeshivah of Radin had brought with them several spools of thread. They were afraid that if so many spools were found in their possession, they might be accused of black market activity. So before the search started, they divided their "hoard" among several other yeshivah student who had no thread at all. After the search had ended and all were back in our barracks, those of us who had received the spools wanted to return them to the two boys from Radin. But the young men refused to take them back. "Keep them as your payment for accepting part of our risk," they said. We were happy at the thought that, despite the subhuman circumstances under which we lived, there were among us men who still retained their qualities of honesty and decency.

AS THE HIGH HOLIDAYS of 5702 (1941) approached, we knew that we would be forced to violate them by working as usual. But

High Holidays in Camp

we refused to ignore the holidays. We had no *shofar*, but we could recite at least some of the holiday prayers while we marched to our work site on the two mornings of Rosh HaShanah. But how were we to do that? Our prayer books had been confiscated. Most of us knew the daily morning service by heart, and some of us could also recite the morning prayer for Rosh HaShanah from memory, but what about *Mussaf*, the additional service that followed morning prayers? *Mussaf* is the most important and solemn part of the Rosh HaShanah service, replete with liturgical hymns which hardly anyone would be able to recite without a *machzor*, the holiday prayer book. Miraculously, one Lithuanian Jew reported to us that his *machzor* had escaped confiscation. We borrowed his *machzor* and copied out the *Mussaf* service, word for word, on scraps of paper, which we gave to the young man who had volunteered to act as cantor.

On both days of Rosh HaShanah we recited *Shacharis*, the morning service, as we marched along the highway and through the woods to our work site. We managed to recite *Mussaf* together also — during our lunch break, hidden from view by two piles of lumber. The student who led the service read the prayers just loud enough for us to be able to repeat them after him. Two other yeshivah students stood guard, watching for camp officials. To be caught praying could have meant death for us. So we had to finish our prayers at top speed, but we recited them with all the more fervor in our hearts, beseeching G-d to grant us another year of life and to give us back our freedom.

ON *SHABBOS SHUVAH*, the Sabbath between Rosh HaShanah and Yom Kippur, we were ordered to roll heavy logs from one place to another. This was hard work, and since we had no gloves, we had to be careful not to injure our hands. Given the conditions under which we lived, even a little scratch could have resulted in a serious infection.

Injured but...Happy

By that time it was late in September and the summer heat had abruptly given way to frigid winter temperatures. Early in the afternoon of *Shabbos Shuvah* one of the logs I was rolling slipped over the tip of my left index finger. Under ordinary circumstances this probably would not have produced much harm, but because my hands and the log were frozen, part of my fingertip came off. Since my hands were numb with cold, I felt no pain at first, but the guard took me to the medic. I was given first aid and released from work for the rest of the day.

Instead of feeling upset at the loss of part of my finger, I was overjoyed at not having to work for at least a few days. That evening, back at the camp, I went directly to the camp clinic. The doctor tidied up the wound, rebandaged it and ordered me to take a whole week off from work. My joy was indescribable when I realized that my week of recuperation would include Yom Kippur. I was only sorry for my friends who would have to work as usual on that most holy and solemn day of the year.

I spent Yom Kippur with a few other Jewish inmates, including Reb Avrohom Tropp, Rosh Yeshivah of the Radin group, who had been ordered not to work on that day because of ill health. Since we did not have a *minyan* (the ten men needed for a formal prayer service), each one of us recited to himself whatever prayers he could remember from the Yom Kippur

Rabbi Avrohom Tropp
זצ"ל

liturgy. Another minor miracle came to pass: one inmate announced that his *Chumash* had not been confiscated, and he read with us the Biblical passages for Yom Kippur. Of course we fasted the whole day, reciting as many prayers as we could, hoping that G-d would hear our cry and grant us a new year better than the past one had been.

The Saturday after Yom Kippur was supposed to be my last day of sick leave. But when I reported at the clinic the surgeon who changed my bandages gave me another three days of freedom. However, he warned me that when those three days had ended, I must report for work without fail. And so, on the following Tuesday, I ceased to be a "privileged character" and rejoined my friends at our work site. It was the second day of the holiday of Sukkos. At least, I told myself, I had been more fortunate than my friends. Thanks to my mutilated finger, I had been able to observe not only Yom Kippur but also the first day of Sukkos.

Farewell to Siberia

OUR WORK BECAME HARDER each passing day, but at least we obtained a little satisfaction from seeing the results of our toil at last. After weeks of uprooting trees, rolling logs and draining swamps, we were promoted to the job of track-laying. We leveled the ground, poured sand over it to make a roadbed, laid the wooden crossties and attached the steel rails to them. One day we had the honor of riding a train over the tracks we ourselves had laid. Our destination: several kilometers deeper into the woods.

We had long forgotten the joy we had felt for our friends who had been released from the labor camp six weeks earlier. We lived only for a minute at a time. Would we ever see the end of our Siberian exile? But we told ourselves over and over again that our deliverance might come when we least expected it.

During the night from Friday to the intermediate Sabbath of Sukkos, there was a sharp knock at the door of our barracks. We awoke in eager anticipation. Our friends had learned of their liberation by a knock on our barracks door at midnight. Could our own day of freedom have come at last?

Two Russian officers entered our barracks and read off a list of names, announcing that the inmates named on the list would be released and shipped out of the camp at once. This time the

These two pictures of the author demonstrate the effects of life in a forced labor camp. At the left, he is shown shortly before the war. At the right, he is shown upon his release from the Rishoti, Siberia, camp in October, 1941, only a bit over two years later

names included that of my brother Berl and myself. It seemed that although we were technically "stateless," the Russians had classified us as Polish citizens.

We were given an hour to pack our belongings and report at the camp entrance. Trembling with joy and relief, we stuffed our few articles of clothing and bedding into the suitcases we had brought with us from Lithuania, and arrived at the camp entrance with plenty of time to spare. Our only sadness now was for those of our friends whose names had not been on the list. I will always remember the look on the faces of those whom we had to leave behind. We could do nothing for them except pray that they, too, would be released before too long. The Siberian winter was already upon us with its full force and only G-d knew how our friends would survive another winter at Labor Camp Number Seven.

I remember giving some of the sugar we still had left from our kind friends in Salock to Gershon Wishniewer, one of the *bachurim* to whom I had come to feel particularly close.

At the camp's entrance, Berl and I, and the other fifty

78 / FROM KLETZK TO SIBERIA

yeshivah students fortunate enough to be released from Labor Camp Number Seven, were met by the camp commander, who parted from us with a formal farewell speech. "*Tovarishi* (Comrades)," he said (as camp inmates, no one had ever dignified us with the title of "Comrade"), "You are free men now. I wish you success, and I hope that you will direct your energies to helping us in our struggle so that we may achieve a great victory over the German murderers."

Later, we learned that, except for two or three individuals, the other yeshivah *bachurim* at Labor Camp Number Seven were released only a week later, but we never saw any of them again. Meir Evier, one of those who remained at the camp, eventually died there from starvation and sheer exhaustion.

After the camp commander had turned on his heel and left us, we joyously strode through the camp gate, out of Labor Camp Number Seven, without so much as one backward glance. Several guards came with us, but this time they did not hold their guns at our backs. They merely escorted us along the highway to a train which they explained would take us to a place "where you may meet some countrymen of yours and join the Polish liberation army."

A Day to Remember

AFTER MONTHS of slave labor and near-starvation we looked like skeletons and felt as weak as kittens — hardly material for freedom fighters, we thought. But we climbed aboard the train, certain that this was one of the happiest days of our lives.

We did not forget that the day was Shabbos, and since it was also the intermediate Sabbath of Sukkos, we launched into a joyous rendition of the *Hallel*, the psalms of praise and thanksgiving, with special emphasis on the seventh verse of Psalm 118: "I shall not die, but live, to declare the wondrous deeds of G-d." We did not care what the other passengers in our car might think of the "songs" we were singing. We were free at last, we told ourselves, and no longer had reason to concern ourselves with the opinions of the Russians. We also hoped most fervently that, with G-d's help, this would be the last time we would be forced to travel on a Shabbos.

Half an hour later our train pulled into the depot of Reshoti, the first stop on the railroad line that linked Vladivostok with Moscow.

We were escorted off the train and taken to the village hall, which was used for conferences, social affairs and dramatic performances. We were informed that this hall would be our home for the next few days while the local authorities registered us and gave us identification cards. Only then would we be permitted to proceed into Russia proper.

Berl and I, along with the others, unpacked our bundles and found ourselves a place to rest our weary bodies. We were served our first meal in freedom: bread (much more than we had ever received at Labor Camp Number Seven) and cheese.

After a while Berl and I decided to take a walk through the village. As in most Siberian villages, the houses in Reshoti were small, with tiny windows. The houses were built half underground to retain as much heat as possible during the cruel Siberian winter. It was still early in October, but temperatures were below freezing and the ground was blanketed with snow.

Berl and I walked along the main street of the village without meeting anyone. The side streets, too, were silent and empty. Despite our meal of bread and cheese, we were still hungry, and so we decided to knock on the door of a house that seemed a little larger and nicer than the others.

An elderly man opened the door. "*Chto chatite?*" (What do you want?) he asked.

We told him that we had just been released from Labor Camp Number Seven, that we were starved and would like to buy some bread. Looking at us with eyes full of compassion, the man replied that bread was scarce in the village; he had barely enough for himself and his family. However, he invited us to come in and offered to give us potatoes and some other vegetables. (We knew that potatoes were a staple available in great abundance even in Siberia, because potatoes need little sunlight.)

As we entered the house, we saw a large pot in which

potatoes were boiling in their skins. The old man offered the potatoes to us and we ate them with relish.

After we had finished eating, our host asked us to describe life at Labor Camp Number Seven. Since we did not know who he might be, we told him only part of the truth. He did not seem surprised by what we told him. Labor Camp Number Seven was only seven miles away from Reshoti, so we probably were not the first labor camp survivors he had seen.

When we were ready to leave, the old man gave us two bags of potatoes to take back with us for our use. We offered to pay him for the potatoes in cash or in goods, but he would not accept any compensation from us.

BY THE TIME we returned to the village hall, it was dark and Shabbos was over. Our friends bombarded us with questions, and when we shared our bags of potatoes with them they literally fell upon us with hugs and kisses.

Hoshana Rabbah

The next day several other yeshivah *bachurim* ventured into the village in search of food.

That night we slept on the floor of the village hall, but it was the first night in many months that we could enjoy the peaceful sleep of free men. We felt we could look to the future with hope and confidence.

Although we did not have to go to work, we awoke very early the next morning because it was Hoshana Rabbah. We had not been able to spend the preceding night in study, as is customary before Hoshana Rabbah, because we did not have any *Gemaras* with us. We also did not have palm and willow branches, but we *davened* together, chanting as many *Hoshana* hymns as we could from memory.

Later that morning we were summoned to the office of the village hall and given instructions how to comport ourselves while we were in Reshoti. "Comrades," a village official said to us, "you are free men now, but you cannot go about freely until you have the proper identification and other required documents. If you leave here and are caught without papers you may be arrested and deported all over again. We are now in the process of

FAREWELL TO SIBERIA / 81

preparing your documents. They will contain your photograph, your name and your age. These documents are not passports. Only citizens of the Soviet Union have the right to own passports. But you must guard your documents carefully because they will be your only identification until you can become citizens of our beloved country."

As soon as the official had finished his talk, we were photographed and told to report at the village hall office the following day to pick up our papers.

That evening we welcomed the festival of Shemini Atzeres with great zeal and emotion. It seemed to us, more than in any other year, "the season of our rejoicing." *Kol atzmosai tomarno;* every part of our bodies sang praises to G-d for having saved us from almost certain death at Labor Camp Number Seven. We realized, of course, that our future was far from secure. We had no place to go and no means of support. Nevertheless, we attempted to forget the hardships and misery of the past months and to concentrate on the hopeful present. Berl and I recited *Kiddush* over two pieces of bread, ate some of our potatoes — raw as they were — and went to sleep.

The next morning, after reciting our prayer and eating the meager breakfast of bread and cheese served us by the village clerk, we went to the village hall office and lined up for our documents. It took two hours until all of us had received our papers. We were told that the valuables we had surrendered to our guards when we had arrived at Labor Camp Number Seven had been sent after us to Reshoti and that we could call for them in a few hours' time.

When we reported to the village hall office again later that day, we received almost everything that had been taken from us at the labor camp — watches, cigarette lighters, and other valuables. Everything, that is, except for our most precious possessions: our *tefillin, talleisim* and prayer books. The Russians had probably destroyed them.

I had come to Labor Camp Number Seven with a cheap wrist watch, but to my surprise I now received a beautiful gold Omega instead. I showed it to all the other *bachurim*, asking them whether the watch belonged to any of them. When no one claimed it, I gladly kept it for myself. Several months later, at Passover time, this watch was to help save Berl and me from starvation.

Because our documents had to state our ultimate destination (in Soviet territory, of course), we had to decide upon a place where we could say we wanted to go. This was a real problem; none of us could name his hometown as his ultimate destination because all these towns had been occupied by the Germans. We had to make a choice: declare our intention to remain in Siberia as free candidates for Soviet citizenship, or move on to more temperate regions such as Kazakhstan, or even farther south to Uzbekistan (which adjoined Kazakhstan) or Tadjiskistan.

AFTER SOME DISCUSSION, all of us (our group then consisted of twenty-five men) decided to head south, because we no longer

We Travel to Kazakhstan

wanted to be burdened by heavy winter clothing, but also because rumors had filtered back to us while we were still in the labor camp that our friends who had been released at the end of August had settled in Dzizak, a small town near Samarkand, in Uzbekistan.

For some reason, unclear to me now, we agreed that we did not want to go to Uzbekistan. We decided to choose between two places. The first was Ayagus, a little town on the railroad line between Novosibirsk and Alma Atta, the capital of Kazakhstan. The second was Chymkent, a larger city in Kazakhstan, near the Uzbekistan border. One group — perhaps a dozen *bachurim* — chose Ayagus. The second group — eight *bachurim* including Berl and myself — opted for Chymkent, on the assumption that yeshivah students were less likely to be noticed and harassed by the Soviet authorities in a large city than in a smaller place.

On Wednesday, the day after the holiday, we picked up our bundles and marched off together to the railroad depot. Two hours late, the Vladivostok-Moscow train arrived. Waving our identification papers as if they were our railroad tickets, we pushed our way into the crowded train. The cars were built

Russian-style. Each car had a long corridor from which doors opened into passenger compartments. Every compartment had two benches, facing each other, each wide enough to accommodate three passengers. At night, two ledges were pulled from the walls; these, along with the benches, provided six berths for sleeping. To us, who had traveled to Siberia packed into boxcars like cattle, the journey out of Siberia seemed as luxurious as a ride on the Orient Express.

With us aboard the train was a group of students from the yeshivah of Radin, who had decided to settle at Merkee, a *kolkhoz* (collective commune) near the town of Dzambul in Kazakhstan.

After many hours, we arrived at Krasnoyarsk, where we remained for an hour. A thick soup made from farina was sold in the station. Of course we all bought the soup and devoured it hungrily, almost in one gulp. But as our stomachs had forgotten how to take in so much food at one time, many of our friends became violently sick. Luckily, my brother Berl and I suffered no ill effects from our hasty meal.

Our train pulled out of the station, traveling farther to the west, until we reached Novosibirsk, a major commercial center.

In Novosibirsk we changed to a train bound southward, for Kazakhstan and Uzbekistan. A young Russian entered the compartment in which Berl and I sat. The youth impressed us with his intelligence. We talked about the never-ending wars, the general political situation, and life under the Soviet system. It was a most interesting conversation. Then the train slowed down and came to a stop at a small depot. Before we knew it, our Russian friend was gone. When the train picked up speed again, we saw that my brother's suitcase, which contained all his clothing and bedding, was gone. The smooth-talking Russian had made off with it. A wise man once asked, "Who is a true swindler?" and answered his own question with the words of Psalmist: "He whose mouth speaks of nothingness and whose right hand is falsehood." This was an apt description of our Russian travel companion. But in the joy of our new freedom, our loss did not upset us too greatly. We truly felt it much later, when we were forced to sell our clothes, piece by piece, to keep from starving.

Continuing south, we eventually arrived at Ayagus. The group that had decided to settle in Ayagus bade us farewell and left the train. We, who had chosen to proceed to Chymkent, were pleased with our choice; judging from the depot, Ayagus seemed to be a most primitive, isolated hamlet.

We stopped at Ayagus for half an hour. During that time Ephraim Zuchovitzky, who was in our group (the Chymkent group), was suddenly stricken with violent cramps and diarrhea and decided to get off at Ayagus.

Our train went on to Alma Atta, the capital of Kazakhstan, where we were told we would have a two-hour stop. We used the opportunity to get off the train and explore the city. We walked for some distance but found nothing of special interest to us except vendors selling apples that had made the city famous ("Alma Atta" means "Father of the Apple"). We bought enough apples at the nearby market place to keep us happy for the remainder of our journey.

Our next stop was Dzambul, where the Radin *bachurim* who were headed for the *kolkhoz* of Merkee parted from us.

Five hours later, we finally arrived at Chymkent. It was Wednesday, October 22, 1941 (1 Cheshvan 5702).

The Jews of Chymkent

WHEN THE EIGHT OF US got off the train at Chymkent, we dropped our bundles near the tracks and joined a long line of people who seemed to be waiting to buy food. When we asked what food was being sold that day, we learned that it was bread, and bought enough to last us for the day.

Two of our friends left us to walk into the center of the city, which was quite a distance from the station, to see whether there were any Jews in Chymkent and to look for possible lodgings.

Meanwhile, the rest of us remained in the station. It was late in the day; we decided that if we found no lodging we should spend the night in the station, but this did not trouble us unduly because it was still summer in Chymkent — many hundreds of miles south of Siberia — and the nights were warm. When it became dark, with no sign of our two friends, we arranged our bundles as mattresses and pillows on the station floor and went to sleep, except for one *bachur*, who stood guard.

The next morning, Thursday, we said our morning prayers quickly, in order not to attract undue attention. After breakfasting on the bread we had bought in the station the day before, we settled down to wait for our two friends to return from their exploration of the city.

It was past noon when they finally came to us with their report. They said there were not many Jews in Chymkent. Of these, only a handful were Ashkenazim, Jews from Eastern Europe like ourselves. The majority seemed to be Bokharan Jews of Sephardic origin, who observed many customs common among Jews in Morocco, Iraq and Yemen.

AMONG THE FEW Ashkenazic Jews in the city was a Lubavitcher *chassid* named Berl Yaffe, who had been exiled to Chymkent with his wife and daughter as a penalty for "seeking to undermine the Soviet system."

Reb Berl Yaffe

It seemed that he had taught children in his hometown to recite, "*Torah tziva lanu Moshe*" (The Torah Moses commanded us is the inheritance of the community of Jacob). The Soviets had thought that in Chymkent, remote from centers of Jewish population, Reb Berl would have no chance to do further "harm." The Yaffe family had now been living in Chymkent for twenty years in virtual isolation, but this only had made Reb Berl even more devout than ever before.

Our friends brought us a message from Reb Berl: We were to come to his home at once with our belongings and be his guests over Shabbos. After Shabbos, he would find us permanent lodging.

The next morning, Friday, after standing on line for another purchase of bread, we cheerfully set out on foot for the Yaffes' home. We were happy to accept Reb Berl's invitation, but we wondered how he would be able to accommodate eight house guests; our friends had told us that the quarters he shared with his wife and daughter had only two rooms. We brought our own food with us; the bread would have to serve us as *challah* for *Kiddush* and also take the place of the fish, the chicken and other delicacies of a normal Shabbos dinner. When we arrived at Reb Berl's place, his wife and daughter welcomed us so warmly that we had difficulty restraining our tears.

Reb Berl was a poor man who eked out a bare subsistence for his wife and daughter by repairing shoes and selling small articles at the village market place. But he had managed to buy a chicken for Shabbos. True, the bird was hardly bigger than a pigeon, but we knew that it represented a substantial outlay of money for Reb Berl.

Eleven people sitting around a small table with only five chairs sounds less than comfortable, but as we sang the *zemiros*, the familiar Sabbath table hymns, we felt as if we were seated in armchairs cushioned with soft plush, and the scrawny chicken that had to feed eleven people for two meals — Friday night and Shabbos noon — tasted as rich and delicious as the main dish of a seven-course dinner at a royal table. We begged our host to share our bread, but Reb Berl and his family firmly refused. When Reb Berl chanted the hymn, *Tzur mi-shelo achalnu...sovanu vehosarnu...*, praising G-d for having given us so much food that we not only could eat our fill but had some left over, we really felt that the words, which were literally untrue, were accurate in spirit. At the end of the meal we recited the Grace after Meals together. Now it was Reb Berl's turn to be deeply moved; he tearfully told us that this was the first time in twenty years that he had been able to *bensh mezuman*, to recite the Grace with the special blessings that can be chanted only when at least three adult Jewish males have broken bread together.

Of course there were no beds for us, and we had to sleep shoulder to shoulder, eight people in one room, but we were so thoroughly saturated with the Sabbath spirit that our sleep was peaceful and sweet.

The next morning we accompanied Reb Berl to the Bokharan synagogue which the Soviet authorities had somehow permitted to survive. We noted that the Bokharans treated Reb Berl with great respect; he occupied the seat of honor at the eastern wall. We were introduced to the *hakham*, the rabbi, who expressed sympathy for our plight.

It was a most interesting experience for us. We had never attended a synagogue service so different from the one we had known in Kletzk and Vilna. We were surprised and happy to see that, even after a quarter-century of Communism, the congregation included not only old men but also younger men and even boys. Here one could see the secret of Jewish survival: unswerving devotion to the Torah.

As we walked home from the synagogue with Reb Berl, he told us of the spiritual loneliness he and his family had suffered for the past twenty years, but he added that they had been sustained and cheered by the thought that whatever sacrifices they had made had all been for the sake of G-d and His Law.

Living as Jews in a Kolkhoz

WHEN WE ARRIVED AT Chymkent, we were only eight yeshivah *bachurim*, but a few days later we were joined by five of our friends who had left the train at Ayagus. Ayagus had been a disappointment; they had found neither Jews nor chance of subsistence. We were now thirteen yeshivah *bachurim* in Chymkent, nine from the yeshivah of Kletzk, three from the yeshivah of Novorodok and one from the yeshivah of Radin. Ephraim Zuchovitzky, who had left the train at Ayagus because of his sudden illness, was not with us. He had died in Ayagus of what had turned out to be dysentery.

Winter was fast approaching and the weather was rainy and unpleasant. We discussed our future with Reb Berl Yaffe. We came to the conclusion that the boys from Radin who had settled at the *kolkhoz* of Merkee had made a wise choice. Contrary to our earlier opinion, we now felt that we would have a better chance of survival in a *kolkhoz* than in a large city. Most of the villages in Kazakhstan were organized as *kolkhozes* or collective communes. There was no private property, except that each family was given a house and a small kitchen garden for its private use. All farming and industry were cooperative, with the *kolkhoz* selling the products of the village on a cooperative basis. Since everyone accepted into a *kolkhoz* was expected to work, the *kolkhoz* made it a rule to find employment for all its members, including, presumably, even such totally unskilled, inexperienced characters as we were. We had come to realize that if we moved to a city where everyone was on his own, we would never find jobs and might eventually be arrested on charges of "parasitism." If we needed more money then the *kolkhoz* could give us, we felt we could always do a little business on the side to augment our income. As it turned out, no one in the *kolkhoz* ever received cash; we were paid in goods, and whatever money we got, we had to obtain through — let us be frank — the black market.

Our choice fell on Mankent, a village about twenty kilometers from Chymkent. We did not want to be too far from Chymkent, because we knew we might have to travel to the city fairly often to do business.

IMMEDIATELY ON OUR ARRIVAL in Mankent, we registered with the *selkom*, the village sheriff's office. We learned that the village consisted not just of one but in fact three separate *kolkhozes*; Chapayev in the center of the village; Stalinkent, to the left of the depot, and Kzeel Yuldus, to the right of the depot. We were also told that there was a serious housing shortage. We were directed to our temporary lodging, a stable that had four sturdy walls but a roof full of holes. Having no other alternative we moved in at once.

Mild Winter, Not for Us

During the night the rain and the cold left us so wet and chilled that even the warm quilts we had brought with us were of no help and we could not sleep.

The next day we heard that in the village near us there lived a Polish-Jewish family of six, the Genats. They only had two rooms, so we could hardly expect them to take us in, but perhaps they would know of a place for us. Anything would be better than our cold, dank stable.

To our amazement, Reb Kalman Genat insisted that we stay with them. "It might be a little crowded with more guests," he admitted, "but at least you would have a warm, dry room in which to sleep."

Still, we were confronted with three immediate problems. First, we had to get ourselves food, because we could not expect the Genats to feed us while we waited to be assigned jobs on the *kolkhoz*. Next, we needed permanent lodgings because we also could not expect the six Genats to remain crowded indefinitely into one room while their other room was filled, literally from wall to wall, with us and our belongings. Finally, we had to locate a place where we could hold daily prayer services with other likeminded Jews, for there was no synagogue in Mankent.

Some of our group went from door to door, begging for bread. The native Kazakhs and Muslims were generally charitable; though they barely had enough bread for themselves, they were glad to share a piece of *lapyoshke*, a kind of pita, with us.

Eventually we were assigned to the cotton fields that were Mankent's principal industry. Our job was to care for the fields until harvest time. A full day's labor brought us a fairly decent ration of bread, but no other food, and no cash to supplement our diet. Those who worked in orchards or in vegetable fields were better off. "Legally" or not, they regularly took some of their produce home with them, while we found the bread increasingly inadequate to pacify our hunger.

After two weeks with the Genats, we found a large room in the *kolkhoz* of Kzeel Yuldus, at the home of a Kazakh by the name of Muhamet Tulamed, who seemed to be an honest man.

Four of us moved into that room: Shlomo Margolis, Moshe Plotnik, my brother Berl, and I. Since there were no beds in the room, we used sacks as mattresses, upon which we placed such pillows and quilts as we had brought from home. Berl and I had to share one quilt because his bedding had been stolen on the train to Chymkent.

HAPPILY, WE DID NOT have too much difficulty organizing religious services for Shabbos, holidays and *yahrzeits*. We found

Our Place of Worship

an Orthodox Jew, a refuge from Pultusk, a little town in Poland, who invited us to use his home as a makeshift synagogue. His name was Bergson. A number of Russian Jews who had fled east to escape the invading Germans joined our congregation. Among them were two refugees from Leningrad, Rav Kantor and Mr. Poliakoff. Rav Kantor, a *shochet*, undertook to discuss the weekly Torah portion at the *sholosh seudos*, the third Sabbath meal held between the afternoon and evening service. Mr. Poliakoff, who had a sweet singing voice, acted as our *baal tefillah*. I still recall his beautiful, heartfelt renditions of the *tefillos* and the *kedushos*.

When the winter began in earnest and our cotton crop had been harvested, we found ourselves unemployed. Nor was there any indication that the *kolkhoz* management would assign us to other work. With our one source of sustenance cut off, we saw the specter of starvation before us. However, we placed our trust in G-d and prayed that He would permit us to live until the war would end and we could either go home or settle in a free country.

We wrote frantic letters to Reb Aharon Kotler in New York, and to Reb Isser Zalman Meltzer and Reb Shneur Kotler in Jerusalem, begging them to find a way of bringing us either to the United States or to Eretz Yisrael. We also asked them to send us food and clothing if that was possible. While waiting for their reply, we went to the village bazaar in search of business opportunities. The bazaar was a gathering place, among others, for other Jews from Poland and Russia who had fled to

Kazakhstan from the battle zones and were now selling a variety of items including old shirts and dresses, soap, matches, lamps and dishes. They told us where we too could find such merchandise for a minimum outlay of cash or barter, and so we, the yeshivah *bachurim*, became peddlers. Most of our merchandise came from Chymkent, twenty kilometers away. To save money and because the train between Chymkent and Mankent did not always go on schedule, we usually made the trip as hitchhikers on passing trucks. Often, we had to walk the entire distance, both ways, with a load of merchandise on our shoulders.

The hunger that was rampant during the winter in Mankent, combined with the unsanitary conditions under which we and the villagers in general lived, caused much illness, particularly typhus and dysentery. When we first arrived in Mankent in the fall of 1941, the Jewish graveyard, a plot of ground donated by the *selkom* for this purpose, contained three graves, children who had died of typhus. By the time we left the village four and a half years later, there were several hundred graves.

OUR GROUP of thirteen yeshivah *bachurim* organized a *chevra kadisha*, a religious burial brotherhood to made sure that the funerals would be conducted in strict accordance with Jewish law. Our work would not only benefit the little Jewish community of Mankent but also — we hoped — give us some desperately needed income from the survivors.

Chevra Kadisha

We divided the work between two groups. Those who had weak muscles but strong nerves performed the *taharah*, the ritual cleansing of the dead. The others, including myself, who were physically strong but too squeamish to handle corpses, dug the graves and closed them after the plain wooden casket had been lowered into place. We bought old white shirts at the bazaar to use as shrouds.

However, our income from peddling merchandise and burying the dead was not enough to sustain us through the winter. We were forced to sell our personal possessions, piece by piece. That winter I sold nearly everything I owned, except for the Omega watch I had received by fortunate mistake from the authorities in Reshoti. I saved that watch as an article of last resort, to be sold only if there was nothing else left to keep Berl and me from starvation.

Our daily diet during the winter of 1941-42 consisted of two meals, breakfast and supper. Breakfast was a large sweet onion. Supper was a concoction of flour boiled in water with a pinch of salt. Today we might use such a mixture as paste for papering our walls, but in Mankent the thick gruel tasted delicious. The onion and the flour paste were our total food intake during twenty-four hours. We could not afford anything else.

To our dismay, we found that we had been too hasty in selling all our Siberian winter clothes. We had to buy old kufaks, short quilted jackets, to replace the overcoats we had sold for bread. The kufaks had to do service not only as overcoats but also as suit jackets, with only a shirt between them and the wearer's bare skin. One kufak, one pair of pants and one pair of high-laced boots lasted us through the winter.

Kazakhstan from the battle zones and were now selling a variety of items including old shirts and dresses, soap, matches, lamps and dishes. They told us where we too could find such merchandise for a minimum outlay of cash or barter, and so we, the yeshivah *bachurim*, became peddlers. Most of our merchandise came from Chymkent, twenty kilometers away. To save money and because the train between Chymkent and Mankent did not always go on schedule, we usually made the trip as hitchhikers on passing trucks. Often, we had to walk the entire distance, both ways, with a load of merchandise on our shoulders.

The hunger that was rampant during the winter in Mankent, combined with the unsanitary conditions under which we and the villagers in general lived, caused much illness, particularly typhus and dysentery. When we first arrived in Mankent in the fall of 1941, the Jewish graveyard, a plot of ground donated by the *selkom* for this purpose, contained three graves, children who had died of typhus. By the time we left the village four and a half years later, there were several hundred graves.

OUR GROUP of thirteen yeshivah *bachurim* organized a *chevra kadisha*, a religious burial brotherhood to made sure that the

Chevra Kadisha

funerals would be conducted in strict accordance with Jewish law. Our work would not only benefit the little Jewish community of Mankent but also — we hoped — give us some desperately needed income from the survivors.

We divided the work between two groups. Those who had weak muscles but strong nerves performed the *taharah*, the ritual cleansing of the dead. The others, including myself, who were physically strong but too squeamish to handle corpses, dug the graves and closed them after the plain wooden casket had been lowered into place. We bought old white shirts at the bazaar to use as shrouds.

However, our income from peddling merchandise and burying the dead was not enough to sustain us through the winter. We were forced to sell our personal possessions, piece by piece. That winter I sold nearly everything I owned, except for the Omega watch I had received by fortunate mistake from the authorities in Reshoti. I saved that watch as an article of last resort, to be sold only if there was nothing else left to keep Berl and me from starvation.

Our daily diet during the winter of 1941-42 consisted of two meals, breakfast and supper. Breakfast was a large sweet onion. Supper was a concoction of flour boiled in water with a pinch of salt. Today we might use such a mixture as paste for papering our walls, but in Mankent the thick gruel tasted delicious. The onion and the flour paste were our total food intake during twenty-four hours. We could not afford anything else.

To our dismay, we found that we had been too hasty in selling all our Siberian winter clothes. We had to buy old kufaks, short quilted jackets, to replace the overcoats we had sold for bread. The kufaks had to do service not only as overcoats but also as suit jackets, with only a shirt between them and the wearer's bare skin. One kufak, one pair of pants and one pair of high-laced boots lasted us through the winter.

Passover in Mankent: 1942

AT LAST, THE WINTER and its chilly rains came to an end. Spring arrives early in Mankent, at the beginning of March. Springtime brought a little relief from hunger. The *kolkhoz* had many fruit trees, from which unripe fruit, hard and green, frequently fell, torn off the branches by the brisk March winds. Starved as we were, we gathered the unripe fruit and ate it greedily. I remember that in one day I ate forty little unripe apples, one after the other. It was a miracle that none of us ever got the dreaded dysentery.

At long last, the *kolkhoz* found new work for us. The Soviet government allowed each *kolkhoz* family a plot of land near their home on which they could plant grain and vegetables. Having no modern agricultural tools, the Kazakhs plowed the soil with their bare hands. We, the yeshivah *bachurim*, were hired to plow the fields by this same incredibly primitive method and then to sow the seeds. Our payments was not cash but a specified quantity of bread and vegetables per day. The work was backbreaking and took the last of our strength. But we were glad to have jobs at all that would help us remain alive.

However, spring brought us new problems, because springtime means that Passover is not far away. Where in this G-d forsaken place would we get the matzoh, the wine and the other Passover foods we would need for the eight days of Pesach? But even as spring brought new life to the frozen soil, so, too, it brought us renewed hope that we would overcome these difficulties even as we had surmounted all the other obstacles of exile in an alien land.

First of all, we needed flour to bake our matzos, but the cost of flour was prohibitive. My brother Berl and I decided that the time had come for us to part with my Omega watch. We bartered it for merchandise, which we sold in the bazaar to get the cash required for the precious flour.

We yeshivah *bachurim* made arrangements to bake our matzos together. Some of us would do the actual baking, which was a delicate operation. One Kazakh family, to whom we explained the importance of this "religious act," kindly permitted us to use their oven for several hours. But when we saw the oven, our hearts sank. The ovens in Kazakhstan were most primitive, very much like the ancient ovens described in tractate *Shabbos* of the Talmud. The oven of our Kazakh friends consisted of a hole in the ground, its sides lined with crude bricks. Instead of wood, which was scarce in that region, turf was used as fuel. The turf was placed in the center of the hole and set on fire. Within minutes, the walls of the oven became extremely hot. The dough was then rolled out into thin sheets which the baker, wearing gloves to protect his hands, plastered onto the oven walls. When the product, which resembled pita, was ready (usually in a matter of moments), the baker tapped it with his gloved hand, so that it fell from the oven walls, ready to eat. Only an expert could perform this job because it was easy to get one's hand burned despite the glove.

Since we knew how unhandy we were, we asked a Kazakh woman to do the baking for us. We brought her the dough we had prepared and explained to her the difference between her pita and our matzos. As we watched, she patted the dough onto the walls of the oven, and moments later, held out a finished matzoh. After a while, one of our friends caught on and started baking matzos by himself. We went to work helping him with great joy, chanting verses from the *Hallel* and other yeshivah melodies from Kletzk.

We apportioned a quota of sixteen matzos for each yeshivah student: one matzoh per meal, two meals a day, for eight days. In addition, we prepared two matzos larger than the others, to be used for the additional quantities that had to be eaten at the *seder*.

DURING THAT PASSOVER season our mood swung back and forth between depression and rejoicing. We were sad when we recalled the past, our hometown, our yeshivah and our fathers and mothers, and when we realized how utterly alone we were in this place which our fathers and grandfathers had not even known existed, among people whose language was not ours, and under a government that knew nothing of G-d and religion. But our spirits lifted when we considered that, despite all the odds against us, we had survived the third winter of the war and were now able to observe the commandment to eat unleavened bread on Pesach.

Matzoh but No Kosher Moror

We now had our matzos, but we were forced to find substitutes for the other ritual foods we needed for the *sedarim*. In place of the four cups of wine we used water, which we had sweetened by cooking dried fruit in it, and I think I enjoyed that thin fruit syrup as much as the choicest Passover wine nowadays. For *karpas* we took white beets, which were plentiful and inexpensive. None of the five species of *moror* (bitter herbs) described in the Talmud could be found in Mankent, but we felt that the bitterness in our own hearts might be an acceptable substitute for the bitter herbs.

I will never forget the meals we ate during that Passover of 1942. For the *sedarim* we had a thick soup prepared from white beets. The beets were so sweet — they were the kind used in the manufacture of sugar — that we could hardly eat them, but we were so hungry that we gulped down the soup nevertheless. Our midday meals consisted of more white beets, this time ground, with a dab of sour cream. But whatever we lacked in food or drink we replaced with spiritual sustenance — lively yeshivah songs and profound Torah discourses that accompanied each meal

Thus we spent Pesach, the festival of our freedom, firmly believing that even as our forefathers had been redeemed from Egypt, so we, too, would live to see our liberation.

Whatever few rubles we earned from our peddling went for food. We did not have enough money left to buy clothes, so our shirts and pants became worn and threadbare. We kept patching the holes with other scraps of material until there were so many patches upon patches that the original material could no longer be recognized.

The Kazakhstan Summer

DURING THE SPRING and summer we walked barefoot to save our shoes for the winter. Summers in Kazakhstan are very hot, and the sandy soil scorched the soles of our bare feet. Fortunately, there were many trees, and we would run from the shade of one tree to that of the next to cool our feet. Frequently we would be barefoot even when we made our twenty-kilometer purchasing trips to Chymkent. We would stop at virtually every tree along the highway to ease the agony of our burning feet in what little shade the trees had to offer.

One summer day, as we walked in the direction of Chymkent, we saw a truck from the *kolkhoz*, laden with red onions, slowly moving ahead of us. Several onions fell from the truck; we picked them up and happily ate them. A man sitting in the back of the open truck saw us. He did not offer us a lift but kept tossing onions to us all the way to Chymkent. We told each other in all seriousness that this man might have been the Prophet Elijah, come in a strange disguise to feed the hungry.

Most of the Russian Jews who lived in Mankent, even though they were refugees from cities and town occupied by the Germans, were better off than we, the yeshivah *bachurim*. They had been able to bring most of their household goods with them. Also, since many of them had been working for government agencies in their hometowns, they obtained government jobs almost immediately on their arrival in Kazakhstan, taking the places of workers who had been drafted into the Red Army. However, they were far from affluent and could not give us much help because their earnings were barely enough for their own needs.

One of our very good friends in Mankent was Mr. Poliakoff from Leningrad, the *baal tefillah* of our Sabbath services at Mr. Bergson's home. One day he invited me to be his guest for Shabbos dinner. I declined the invitation, explaining that I did not want to come to his home barefoot and dressed in the one pair of pants I owned, because they were in a deplorable condition. But Mr. Poliakoff refused to take no for an answer, pointing out that, unfortunately, there were hundreds of Jews whose wardrobes were no better than mine. And so I accompanied him to his home after morning services. The meal was simple, of course, but the Shabbos spirit was very much alive, and whatever the food lacked was more than offset by the warm family atmosphere that surrounded me at the Poliakoffs. Thereafter, I was a regular Shabbos guest at the Poliakoff home.

Sorrows and Joys

AS SPRING MOVED TOWARD summer and the holiday of Shevuos came closer, we were once again in despair. We had no food, no possibility of earning a few extra rubles and virtually no possessions left to sell. I lay down on the floor of our room alongside my brother and sighed, "Berl, what are we to do now? We can only hope for a miracle."

Berl took a walk to the *chaychana* or "tea house," a cabin in the center of the *kolkhoz* where people usually gathered to listen to the radio, to meet friends and to discuss the events of the day. The *chaychana* was our one link with the world outside.

In a short while, Berl returned, out of breath and flushed with excitement. "You got your miracle, Alter!" he shouted exultantly. He had learned that three food packages were on the way to us from America, via Teheran. They had been sent from New York by our beloved Rosh Yeshivah, Reb Aharon Kotler. With G-d's help, said Berl, these packages should be in our hands before long.

We rushed out to tell the good news to the others. On the strength of the promised packages from America we borrowed some money, bought a large loaf of bread, and enjoyed what we considered a veritable feast on Shevuos.

It was a good feeling for us to know at last that Reb Aharon had received our letter, that he knew where we were, and that he was in a position to send us help.

The packages from New York arrived in Mankent soon after Shevuos. They contained tea, cocoa, saccharin and other staple foods. We were amazed that people in American seemed to know exactly what was needed in Kazakhstan. The most sought-after commodity was tea, which, the Kazakhs claimed, was of even greater importance than bread because it prevented headaches and a host of other ailments. The Kazakhs were willing to give anything for a package of tea. Saccharin was another precious item because sugar was scarce in Mankent. We could sell one saccharin tablet for two rubles; a bottle of 1,000 tablets brought us the incredible sum of 2,000 rubles.

Two weeks later we received nine more packages from New York, with badly needed clothing: pants, shirts and shoes. The packages were not all addressed to the same individual, but the person who received a package addressed to him knew that its contents were meant to be divided equally among all the other *bachurim*.

FROM THAT TIME ON we received packages on a virtually regular basis and our lives began to assume a semblance of normalcy. The contents of the packages gave us a feeling of independence because we could use them as barter for food we needed badly, including potatoes, which were very expensive.

Hope For a Better Future

As for the clothes, they were a G-dsend, for until then, each of us had only one shirt which he had to wear until it was unbearably dirty and he could no longer delay washing it. While it dried, its owner had to go about half-naked.

Our new sense of physical well-being gave us sufficient peace of mind to resume our studies, which we had shamefully neglected for many months. One of our friends had been able to save two *seforim* from confiscation by the Russians: the first volume of the *Midrash Rabbah* and one copy of the Talmudic tractate *Pesachim*. My friend Michel Malachovsky and I began to study *Pesachim* together and were able to complete the entire tractate. (Rabbi Malach[ovsky] was later the rabbi of a Bronx congregation; he died in 1978.)

Meanwhile, we gave thought also to the future. Good news had begun to come from the battlefront. Early in February, 1943, a news broadcaster, his voice throbbing with exultation, announced a great Russian victory at Stalingrad: Hitler's entire Sixth Army had been annihilated. From that time on, each day brought new reports of German withdrawals on all fronts as city after city, town after town, was recaptured by the Red Army.

Once again, our hoped soared. There seemed to be a strong possibility that our hometown, Kletzk, would be liberated soon and that the Russians would allow us to return to our families. At the time we were still totally unaware that the loved ones with whom we hoped to be reunited in Kletzk were no longer there and, in many instances, also no longer alive. We did not know that entire Jewish populations of towns and cities had been gunned down by Nazi firing squads.

Each morning we awoke early, *davened*, ate our meager breakfast and then rushed off to the *chaychana* for the latest war bulletins. We would listen intently for the names of cities retaken by the Soviets during the previous night. We heard names familiar to us: Vitebsk and Smolensk on the northern front, and Kiev and Kharkov in the South.

And so the months passed until the beginning of 1944 when, at long last, we heard the announcer read from his list of liberated areas the cities closest to our hearts: Vilna, Lida, Slonim, Baranovice, Nesves, Lachovice and Kletzk.

By that time we had gathered that most of the Jews in Lithuania had been annihilated. We looked at one another, each with the same unspoken thoughts. Had our families survived? Berl and I spent restless days and sleepless nights thinking of our parents, our sisters Rochel and Shulamis, our brother Mordechai, and all our other relatives. We could not believe that they all could be dead.

Finally Berl and I decided to write to the *gordspolkom* (town hall) of Kletzk, asking information about the fate of our family. After mailing the letter we waited impatiently for the reply.

Several months later, we received an answer from Kletzk. "The names of the persons concerning whom you have inquired are not in our registry," the letter read. "The Germans killed all the Jews in Kletzk. One group of over 4,000 was shot on October 30, 1941. The 850 Jews who were not killed in that mass shooting were interned in a ghetto, which was liquidated nine months later, on July 19, 1942. Only a handful of Jews escaped. Their names are not known to us."

All our other friends who had written letters of inquiry to their hometowns received much the same tragic news as Berl and I. Only our roommate Moshe Plotnik was informed that one of his sisters had survived.

When we understood at last what had probably happened to our family, Berl and I wept bitterly, but we could not observe a *shivah* for our loved ones, because we had no eyewitness reports of their deaths. There was always a shadow of a chance that at least some of them had managed to escape the Nazi murderers and were still alive somewhere.

The enormity of the fate that had befallen the Jews of Europe left us so stunned with shock and grief that, for a while, we were incapable of thinking and behaving rationally. But the urge to survive won out and we pulled ourselves together, each attempting to console the others, to pick up the threads of our lives and continue our struggle to endure until Hitler would go down in final defeat.

STRANGELY, THE SOVIET government was much more tolerant of our religious life, and of our illegal trade with the contents of our food packages, than it probably would have been under normal conditions. Even in the best of times food had not been abundant in the Soviet Union. But during the war years, food lines were interminably long and there were never enough groceries for all those waiting. Without the trading activities of the kind we carried on, many people

Tolerance from the Soviet Government

SORROWS AND JOYS / 103

would have starved. And so the Soviet authorities looked the other way. It was possible to obtain anything on the black market, provided one had the money. Even government employees turned to the black market for their everyday needs, but they made certain that no one should know they were doing it.

On one occasion, as I was walking about in the bazaar trying to find a customer for an oil lamp, a young gentile approached me and asked to have a look at the lamp. He told me that he was a police officer and wanted to buy it. He explained that since he had no cash with him, he was unable to pay me. However, he insisted on taking the lamp with him, saying that I should report at the police station at three o'clock that afternoon, at which time I would be paid.

I was badly frightened. Was this a trap? Should I go to the police station or should I write off the lamp as a loss? After discussing the matter with my friends, it was decided that I should report at the police station as instructed to collect my money. If the officer had wanted to arrest me for illegal trading activities, my friends pointed out, he could have done so on the spot without pretending to make a purchase from me, but if, contrary to their expectations, I would find myself facing charges of black market trading, I should sincerely explain to the police that the lamp had been my personal property and that I had been forced to sell it in order to buy bread.

I reported at the police station at three o'clock that afternoon. The officer was there and really paid me, not in cash but with a pound of potatoes. Although the lamp was worth much more, I walked out happily with my potatoes, grateful for my escape.

Also much to our surprise, the Soviet authorities in Mankent showed remarkable forbearance in their attitude toward our religious activities. Only once, on the second day of Rosh HaShanah, 1943, just as our *baal tefillah*, Mr. Poliakoff, began the repetition of the *Shemoneh Esrei* prayer, the local chief of police entered the room at Mr. Bergson's place where the service was held and angrily ordered us to leave. It seemed that two days of religious services had been a bit too much for the Russians. We quickly scattered in every direction, grateful to G-d that we had not been placed under arrest. But as a rule, the Soviets did not attempt to disrupt our religious services although they were aware that these were conducted on a regular basis.

Happiness in Our Midst

OUR LIVES WERE NOW relatively free from material concerns because we continued to receive food and clothing packages via Teheran, first from Reb Aharon and his friends in New York and later also from Reb Aharon's son Reb Shneur and from Reb Isser Zalman Meltzer in Jerusalem. We were able to buy bread each day and to change into clean clothes whenever that was necessary. Nevertheless, we were lonely and unhappy. We could not forget that our families were probably gone and that we were, each of us, alone in the world. It was clear that the Germans were losing the war. But once the war was over, where could we go, and to whom?

One summer day in 1944, we were startled to learn that the youngest student in our group, who was then about twenty-one years old, had become engaged. His bride-to-be was the daughter of refugees from the German-occupied sector of Russia. Preoccupied with the problems of survival, most of us had never even thought of marriage, although we all were by then well within the "eligible" age. The news of our friend's engagement brought us face to face with a new reality: the only way for us to resume a normal life after the war would be to get married and establish families of our own as soon as possible to replace the family circles we had lost.

A few weeks later we celebrated our friend's wedding. The marriage ceremony was conducted by Rav Kantor, whose erudition in Jewish matters entitled him, under Jewish law, to act as *mesadar kiddushin* (celebrant) at marriages. There was not much food, but plenty of enthusiastic singing and dancing, and heartfelt speeches wishing the newlyweds a happy future together.

A short time after that wedding, just before Rosh HaShanah, another member of our group got married to one of the Jewish Mankent girls. Thank G-d, our yeshivah family was growing.

My Wedding

A SHORT DISTANCE NORTH of Mankent there was a little village called Sastube, which had only one landmark, its railroad depot. During the war years, Sastube's native population of Central Russian peasants had been augmented by many Polish Jews who had been released from Siberian labor camps but had not felt any particular desire to join the Polish liberation army. Each day, two passenger trains passed through Sastube: the Novosibirsk-Tashkent train and the Moscow-Tashkent train. There were also several freight trains.

The Jews of Sastube drew their meager income from the passengers of the trains during their brief stops in the village. The Jews bought fruit and vegetables at the bazaar to sell to the passengers, either for cash or for articles which they later sold again at the bazaar.

On the Sunday morning before Yom Kippur, 1944, while we had our daily morning services at Mr. Bergson's place, a bearded man and a young girl entered the room which served as our temporary synagogue. They received a warm welcome from the Bergsons. After the service, Mr. Bergson introduced the visitors to us: Reb Yeshaya Fischerman and his daughter Esther, from Sastube. The Fischermans, we learned, were Polish Jews, originally from Prossnitz, a small town near Warsaw. Earlier in the war, the Bergsons and the Fischermans had spent some time together in a Siberian labor camp. Mr. Fischerman told us that he had been trying to organize a *minyan* for Yom Kippur services and needed someone who could lead the congregation in the *Mussaf* service. He had therefore come to Mankent in the hope of persuading one of our yeshivah students to perform that important function in Sastube. Somehow, Mr. Fischerman's choice fell on me.

I went to my room at once, packed my belongings and joined the Fischermans for the forty-five-minute train journey to Sastube. At the Fischerman home I was greeted warmly by the rest of the family — Mrs. Fischerman, two other daughters, two sons, one son-in-law and a small grandchild.

That Yom Kippur I not only conducted the *Mussaf* service but also led the Jews of Sastube in the *Kol Nidrei* and evening service of the night before, and in *Neilah*, the solemn but joyful concluding service. Mr. Fischerman himself acted as cantor for *Shacharis* and *Minchah*, the morning and afternoon services, respectively.

When I left Sastube for the return trip to Mankent the day after Yom Kippur, the whole Fischerman family escorted me to the depot. The son-in-law, Hertzka Schmeiser, walked with me ahead of the others. "Are you interested in getting married?" he asked me (rather bluntly, I thought). "If you are, would you consider marrying my sister-in-law Rivka?" Rivka was the third of the Fischerman daughters, a pretty, dark-haired girl of nineteen.

I was taken completely by surprise. I liked the family, I had enjoyed being with the young people, but I had hardly spoken two words to Rivka alone. But I did not want to offend the Fischermans. So I mumbled, "I would need time to think it over." Mr. Schmeiser understood my embarrassment and we parted as good friends.

Back in Mankent, I spent some sleepless nights wondering what to do about the Fischermans and Rivka. Should I get married at all while my own situation was still so unsettled, or should I wait until I had found a permanent home where I could rebuild my life? The recent marriages of my two friends helped me make up my mind. I decided to marry as soon as possible, and

I resolved to become better acquainted with Rivka Fischerman.

Our group spent a happy Sukkos. With the permission of our Kazakh landlord, Berl, our roommates and I built a *sukkah* in the back yard. We had neither *lulavim* nor *esrogim* but we hoped that the war would be over soon, and that before too long we would be able to reestablish ourselves in Jewish communities where religious observances would be no problem.

Two weeks after Sukkos we were startled by a summons from the *selkom*. We were to report for duty in the "Working Army," the auxiliary corps that assisted the soldiers on the battlefront. Our initial reaction was dismay. What were we to do? But then we learned that this mobilization was not district-wide; it was only in our village. So we thirteen students decided to leave Mankent for a while in hopes that the *selkom* would forget about us. This was not wishful thinking. Mankent had no shortage of manpower for the "Working Army"; moreover, the local bureaucracy was in such a state of disorganization that the officials of one village had not the slightest idea of what their counterparts in neighboring localities were doing. My brother Berl and the others left for Chymkent, but I saw my draft notice as the "finger of G-d." I decided to take temporary refuge with the Fischerman family in Sastube.

The Engagement Party

I HAD PLANNED to postpone my decision about Rivka for at least another month, and I knew that going to Sastube would force me to decide one way or another. But now it seemed to be the will of G-d that I should marry Rivka Fischerman.

The Fischermans received me with open arms as if I had already become part of the family. During the two weeks I spent at their home, I came to love them all. I was particularly impressed with the beautiful relationship between the Fischerman parents and their children. By the time I received word that the "storm had blown over" in Mankent, I had made my decision. When Hertzka Schmeiser approached me again on Rivka's behalf, my answer was a firm, "Yes."

Mr. & Mrs. Yeshaya Fischerman

I returned to Mankent as a happy bridegroom-to-be. Several weeks later, on the third night of Chanukah, I was back in Sastube, accompanied by my brother Berl and several other *bachurim* from our group, to celebrate my engagement to Rivka. The evening at the Fischermans was filled with laughter, song, good food (the best that my future mother-in-law had been able to buy and prepare), and heartfelt good wishes.

The weeks that followed were exciting and joyful. I spent most of the winter of 1944 to 1945 commuting between Mankent and Sastube.

Several months later, Berl followed my example. He became engaged to Sarah Mazurek, from Kurenice near Vilna, who had come to Mankent with her family as refugees from the German invasion.

In December, 1944, Berl and I received a postcard from New York. It was from Reb Aharon Kotler himself, the first direct communication we had received from anyone outside Russia since the winter of 1940, when we had first learned of Reb

Aharon's safe arrival in the United States. The Rosh Yeshivah wrote:

> Dear Friends Moshe Chaim* and Berl Pekier,
>
> I am surprised that you have not written to me to acknowledge receipt of the packages we have been sending to you from New York once each month. We also sent you packages by way of Teheran and Eretz Yisrael, and even money to be divided equally among all our friends. Why haven't you written to me or to my son Shneur? Have you any news from your family? We are doing everything we can to help you. With the help of our Father in Heaven, we shall all soon witness the deliverance of the Jewish people.
>
> I wish you good health and good luck. Regards to all the friends who are with you. Be well.
>
> Your friend, who will not forget you,
Aharon Kotler

As we read Reb Aharon's message, our eyes filled with tears of joy. As a matter of fact, we had sent many postcards and even letters to Reb Aharon in New York and to Reb Shneur in Jerusalem, but they obviously had not received most of our communications. We had received some money from New York, but we had answered that we did not want any more money. For each one hundred American dollars sent us by Reb Aharon's affluent friends in New York, the Russians gave us one hundred and ten rubles, which could buy just eight pounds of bread, while American goods worth the same amount in dollars could earn us thousands of rubles when we sold them.

The packages from New York and Jerusalem had accomplished a minor miracle for us, the yeshivah students. Aside from enabling us to eat and dress better, they had gained us the respect of the villagers, including many non-religious Jewish refugees in Mankent, who eagerly bought what we had to sell. People who previously had ridiculed us as fanatics stupid enough to go hungry rather than work on Shabbos now praised us as

---

* Although I have always been called by the nickname Alter by my family and friends, the *Rosh Yeshivah* addressed me here by the name which I received at my *bris* and by which I am called to the Torah.

The post card from Reb Aharon

smart, successful young men who not only stood firmly by their religious principles but also had good brains for business.

THE NEWS FROM the fighting fronts continued to be favorable. We stayed glued to the radio in the *chaychana*. When it was

MY WEDDING / 111

Good News from the Front reported that, at last, the Allied forces were fighting the Germans on their own soil, we knew that Hitler's end was near.

On Tuesday, May 8, 1945, we were awakened by excited shouts from the street. "The war is over! The German army has surrendered to the Allies!" Young and old, Jews and gentiles took to the streets of the village, cheering wildly, dancing and singing patriotic songs until late into the night.

Rivka Fischerman and I were married exactly two weeks later, on May 22, 1945 (10 Sivan 5705), at the home of Mr. and Mrs. Bergson, our good friends whose home we used as a *shul*. Our marriage, too, was solemnized by Rav Kantor. In keeping with the precept that one should not celebrate two joyous events at the same time, Berl and his fiancee, Sarah, waited a week before they, too, celebrated their wedding. They were married in Chymkent, at the home of Reb Berl Yaffe, the Lubavitcher *chassid* who had so generously befriended us when we had first arrived from Siberia three and a half years earlier. There were many speeches at both weddings, and much singing and dancing. The "native" Russian Jews, with their hearty and enthusiastic manner, added a unique flavor to both our *simchos*. A quarter-century later, at the weddings of my own children in New York, I honored the young couples with the same songs that these wonderful Jews had sung for Rivka and me.

Now we waited impatiently for permission to return to our hometowns, but we were told that this would take some time. Due to the shortage of railroadcars, a mass "repatriation" of Polish refugees from Soviet territory (there were over 100,000 of them) was impossible. As it turned out, we had to wait ten months to leave Mankent. During that time we tried to remain calm and busied ourselves with preparations for the journey home. I spent much time commuting between Sastube, where Rivka and I now lived, and Mankent, where I still studied with the other yeshivah *bachurim*.

We began to receive news from our lucky friends of the Mirrer yeshivah who had been able to leave Russia earlier in the

Alter and Rivka Pekier after their wedding

war. We had heard nothing from them over the years. Now we learned that most of them had settled in Shanghai. I immediately dispatched a postcard to Shanghai, in care of my friend Abraham Aaron Malinowitz (now a rabbi in Manhattan), telling him how we had fared and that almost all of us were now married, or engaged, or at least actively in search of brides. I wrote to Abraham that our marriages had been motivated by the same thoughts that had inspired our patriarch Isaac, whose marriage to Rebeccah brought him comfort after the death of his mother, Sarah. After losing our loved ones in the Holocaust, our marriages, too, gave us strength and courage to make meaningful lives for ourselves.

As I later learned, my postcard set off great excitement among our friends in Shanghai. They had not known whether we had survived or whether we had perished in Siberia, and they were overjoyed that we were not only alive but were establishing new families of our own.

MY WEDDING / 113

We Leave the Soviet Paradise

BEFORE WE KNEW IT, the summer of 1945 had passed and Rosh HaShanah was upon us. During those solemn days, the first High Holiday season after the war, our hearts were filled with gratitude to G-d for having kept us alive. Our only prayer now was that we should not have to stay too long in Russia but could soon go about the business of finding new homes. At Sukkos we rejoiced in anticipation of freedom. This time the approaching winter held no more terror for us, because we now had warm suits, coats and even gloves to protect us from the chill and rain.

Much to our disappointment, Chanukah found us still sitting on our bundles, waiting for the word that we could leave at last. For the first time since the war, we celebrated Chanukah as we had done at home. We now had the heart to make *dreidels* for the traditional Chanukah game and to bake hot *latkes*. Someone even located a camera (owned by one of the refugee families) and ten of us, yeshivah students in Mankent, posed for a group picture that is still with us as a precious memento.

Purim, 1946, was a particularly happy holiday for us, because we received word that our repatriation would begin in

Chanukah, 1946. A group of yeshivah students awaiting their liberation from Siberia. Bottom row, l. to r.: Moshe Plotnik ז״ל, Shlomo Margolis, David Meir Tzibuch ז״ל, Michel Malach ז״ל, Alter Pekier. Top row, l. to r.: Berl Pekier ז״ל, Leizer Milstein, Avigdor Offen, Shmuel Maslow, Nochum Zeldes

three weeks' time. As we listened to the reading of the *Megillah* we enthusiastically banged and thumped floors and tables at each mention of the wicked Haman and in our minds pronounced juicy Russian curses upon the Hamans of the present day. We had managed to get some good Russian vodka to observe the Purim custom of drinking until we no longer knew the difference between "Blessed be Mordechai" and "Cursed be Haman."

When we received our travel instructions, we realized that we would probably have to observe Passover aboard a train. To prepare for that eventuality, we baked large quantities of matzos in the primitive Kazakh ovens and laid in a stock of potatoes and other foods needing no special preparation for Passover.

On April 10, 1946, we were informed that a train with seats reserved for repatriates would pass through Mankent the following day and that we should report to the station early in the morning with our belongings to meet the train. We slept little that

WE LEAVE THE SOVIET PARADISE / 115

Matzoh baking in Mankent, Kazakhstan, 1946

night, fearful lest we oversleep and miss our chance of freedom. At eight o'clock the next morning we were at the station, but the train did not arrive until four o'clock that afternoon. At six o'clock the train left Sastube, where it had taken on additional repatriates, including Rivka's whole family. Two hours later, we arrived in Chymkent, where we stayed for two days waiting for other Polish refugees, Jews and gentiles, from the surrounding localities.

Two days before Passover — it was a Saturday night — our transport, dozens of wagons long, steamed out of the station, with hundreds of happy voices raised in song. The cars in which we traveled back to freedom were the same type of boxcars which carried us to Siberia five long and bitter years earlier. But now we were free: the doors of our cars were wide open and the windows unobstructed by bars.

We spent the *sedarim*, and the rest of Passover, aboard the train. In our boxcar there were twenty-five single persons and ten families. Each family made its own *seder* so that we had, in the one boxcar, ten separate *sedarim* going on at the same time. Bundles and sleeping benches served as *seder* tables. Each family recited the *Haggadah* softly to themselves, but when we came to the familiar songs and hymns, everyone joined in a harmony of sheer delight. Even the hissing of the locomotive and the squeak of the train wheels as they rolled over the tracks seemed to be keeping tune with our music. We felt as if all of Creation were singing with us and sharing our joy as we traveled toward freedom.

To remind ourselves that under normal circumstances travel is forbidden on *Yom Tov*, we did not leave our cars at the station stops during the first two and last two days of Passover, but on Chol HaMoed, the intermediate days, when travel is permitted, we got off every time the train stopped, which was quite often. This was our first opportunity to observe "normal" life in Russia. Traveling thousands of miles through scores of Soviet towns and cities, we saw the complete lack of organization that hampered the marketing of products. In one town there was a surplus of one product and few purchasers, so that the product was sold at an incredibly cheap price, while in a town only five hours away, we saw that the same product was scarce but in great demand and sold at exorbitant prices.

Most of the train stops were not passenger stations but nondescript freight terminals without signs. We later learned that this had been planned on purpose by the Communists, who did not want the Polish repatriates to make extensive contacts with local inhabitants. Hence we knew that we were passing through such major cities as Kharkov and Kiev only when a train official happened to mention it afterwards. At one point we crossed a long bridge over a wide river. We assumed that this had to be the Volga. "We're back in Europe again, thank G-d!" we exclaimed.

AFTER SEEMINGLY ENDLESS DAYS of traveling, our train came to a stop and the conductor shouted, "Sarna!" Excitedly, we

Passover on the Train

leaped to the door of our boxcar for the first time since the summer of 1941, we were passing through a familiar Jewish *shtetl*. We stopped at Sarna for only ten minutes. A short time later our train pulled into Kovel, a famous Jewish community near the new Russian-Polish border. Here, we were told, we would have a layover of several hours because of customs and other legal

WE LEAVE THE SOVIET PARADISE / 117

formalities. After leaving Kovel we would be out of the Soviet Union and under Polish jurisdiction.

We left the train to explore the city. On our way to Kovel's main synagogue, we passed German prisoners of war, guarded by Russian troops and doing hard labor. This was the first time we had ever seen German soldiers, because the Germans did not occupy our hometown, Kletzk, until after we ourselves had left. By the grace of G-d, the Russians had taken us away before we could fall into the hands of the Nazis. As we saw the sad remnants of Hitler's *Wehrmacht* in their defeat and degradation we shouted curses at them, but unfortunately this could not bring back the millions of Jews whom the Germans had brought to death.

Tears streamed from our eyes and our bodies shook with sobs as we walked through Kovel's once proud and beautiful Great Synagogue. We had already learned from local newspapers in Chymkent that the Germans had herded all the Jews of Kovel into that synagogue before taking them to the execution site where they were shot. The walls of the synagogue were covered with handwritten messages and prayers written by the Jews before the Germans had escorted them to their death. There were countless signatures, including names of entire families. Passages from the prayer book such as "Our Father, our King, avenge the blood of Thy servants that has been shed!" were interspersed with heart-rending appeals: "World, why are you silent?" "Dear Jews, avenge our deaths" and "Remember! Never forget!"

We filed out of the synagogue in stricken silence. On our way back to the train station we met no Jews at all but we stopped several gentiles and asked them to tell us what had become of the Jews of Kovel. Without exception, the gentiles turned their heads from us in silence or mumbled evasive replies.

When our train was half an hour out of Kovel, Polish soldiers entered our car. "*Dzen dobry wam!*" they said. "A good day to you!" We had never particular loved the Polish language, because the Poles had never been our friends, especially not during the years between the two World Wars, but now the Polish words were sweet music to our ears because they meant that we had left the Soviet hell behind us at long last and could look to the future with a little more hope.

Our train pulled into the city of Lublin, noted throughout the Jewish world before the war as the seat of Yeshivas Chachmei Lublin. Here, when we got off the train, we met Jews in the station. They gave us an emotional welcome and told us many things we had already suspected about the fate of Polish Jewry. In Lublin, the Polish gentile repatriates who had boarded the train at Sastube left us because they had reached their final destination. We Jews, who did not know where our journey would end, bade the Poles a cordial farewell. They, in turn, said they hoped we would soon be able to find new homes. After they had gone, we climbed into our boxcars again for the next stage of our journey into the future.

From Lublin, our train moved deeper into Poland, toward Warsaw and Lodz. We did not know the ultimate destination of our train, or where we ourselves wanted to go. Rivka and I decided that the best place for us to settle, at least temporarily, would be some Polish city where we could expect to find other Jews who had survived the Holocaust and with whom we could discuss where to go next.

Lodz

WHILE RIVKA AND I were talking, two yeshivah *bachurim* from the next car came to us and told us that our next stop would be Lodz. When our train pulled into Lodz twenty minutes later, we saw a group of yeshivah *bachurim* waiting on the station platform. As soon as our train stopped, the young men clambered aboard our boxcar. They said they were students of a yeshivah of Holocaust survivors that had been organized in Lodz and that they were meeting every transport of repatriates, urging all yeshivah students and other Orthodox Jews to get off the train and stay in Lodz at least temporarily. The committee which supported the yeshivah would provide for our material needs also. Under the circumstances, my wife and I felt that this would be an ideal opportunity for us to rest a while and to gather strength for our next move.

Rivka's family did not want to come with us. They said that they would rather continue their journey and leave the train only wherever all the other Jewish repatriates would get off. We were reluctant to part from them, but we felt certain that we would meet again soon.

We were urged to hurry because the train was to stop in Lodz for only half an hour, but this did not concern us too much. Except for the few articles of clothing we had bought during our final months in Kazakhstan, we had hardly any baggage.

After hurried farewells to the Fischermans and our friends, Rivka and I, together with another friend and fellow student, Shmuel Maslow and his young wife, left the boxcar that had been our home for three weeks. The yeshivah *bachurim* who had met our train took us to a building on Zachodnia 66 where the yeshivah had settled.

From the isolation and hardships of Kazakhstan we now entered a new world of freedom and bustling activity at Zachodnia 66. As we passed through the entrance of the building with our meager belongings, we saw young men and women, dressed in good clothes that looked quite new, milling about in the hallway. They all greeted us warmly. Some of them were repatriates from Russia like ourselves. Others were survivors of the death camps: Auschwitz, Bergen-Belsen and Treblinka. The young women were the brides of the students. In Lodz, too, the yeshivah survivors had married quickly in order to replace the families they had lost.

WE NOTED THAT Zachodnia 66 was not just one building but a compound of several tall buildings surrounding a courtyard, into which the rear doors of all the buildings opened. The front entrances of some of the buildings opened on Piotrkovski Street, the city's main thoroughfare. Zachodnia 66 had become home to almost all the Orthodox Jews who had come to Lodz from Hilter's concentration camps and Soviet labor camps. In addition to the yeshivah and quarters for the students and their wives, the compound housed a shelter for Orthodox girls run by B'nos Agudath Israel (the girls' organization of the World Agudath Israel movement), a mikveh and the main offices of the Jewish community. There were even two dining halls, one for yeshivah students (it was managed by Leib Greenspan, a member of the Radin group, who died in New York in the 1970's). These dining halls, in which three meals were served each day, were used mainly by single persons, although there were also some married couples who had not yet been assigned housekeeping facilities of their own.

The committee assigned us sleeping quarters and gave us money to buy new clothes. When we asked from where all this bounty had come, we were told that the entire operation had been made possible by funds sent from the United States by the Vaad

Hatzalah, which had been founded to rescue and assist Orthodox rabbis and rabbinical students and their families whose special religious needs were not always adequately met by the larger Jewish relief organizations.

All the activities that went on at Zachodnia 66 were supervised by Rabb Mordechai Zuckerman and his wife, under the guidance of the rabbi of Lodz, Rabbi Kravitz. Rabbi Kravitz, who had survived the death camps, dedicated all his energies to the repatriates from the Soviet labor camps. His door was always open to anyone in need of comfort or advice. He kept a gentile at his home every Shabbos to answer emergency telephone calls and to go into action wherever help could not wait until the Sabbath had ended. Rabbi Kravitz was a man of legendary humility. Because he was so self-effacing, he never appeared in public, and we never had the privilege of meeting him and expressing our appreciation to him in person.

Our stay in Lodz was to be short — only three months, from the beginning of May until the end of July, 1946. Yet even now, forty years later, I look back upon this period as the most interesting and exciting time of my life. Each day brought new arrivals, men and women who had miraculously emerged from the Holocaust, bruised in spirit but alive and ready to resume a normal existence. There were emotional family reunions as brothers, sisters, cousins, parents and children, who had thought one another dead, fell into each other's arms. There were tears, but were tears of joy. It was a wonderful time.

Despite our happiness and relief, Rivka and I spent sleepless nights thinking about our future. We hoped to make our way to western Europe — France, Belgium, Holland or Great Britain — from where we could eventually move on to America or to Eretz Yisrael.

NOW, FOR THE FIRST TIME, we heard, over and over again, the number "six million." We heard, for the first time, that more than **Six Million** one-third of our people had been exterminated by the Nazis. We also learned about the revolt that had taken place in the Warsaw Ghetto during the

Passover season of 1943, and about countless other, less-known acts of Jewish heroism. We visited the *balut*, a neighborhood which, before the war, had been inhabited mainly by what had been described as the Jewish "proletariat." During the war, the *balut* had become the ghetto of Lodz. Now, only empty shells of houses with burned-out chimneys remained. We could hardly bear to look at this new reminder of our tragedy. With tears blurring our vision, we stood for a few moments in mournful silence and them started back for Zachodnia 66, quietly humming a new melody we had learned: *Ani Ma'amin*,* which many thousands of Jews had sung during the days of the Nazi terror, even as they marched to their death in the gas chambers.

Now, too, for the first time, my brother Berl and I learned exactly what had happened to our parents, our sisters Rochel and Shulamis, and our younger brother Mordechai. On one single day, the ninth day of Cheshvan 5702 (October 30, 1941), the Germans massacred 4,500 Jews in Kletzk. The helpless Jews — men, women and children — were driven to sand pits at the foot of Neshvitz Street, where they were mowed down by machine guns, fifty at a time. In the confusion, three Jews had managed to escape. One of them, Shaya Koshetzky, told us that our parents, our two sisters and our brother had been among the people he had last seen at the sand pits.

And yet, the atmosphere at Zachodnia 66 was one of pulsating life. Since all of us were literally sitting on our bundles waiting for opportunities to move on, our existence during those three months in Lodz could hardly be described as stable. But somehow, our lives were orderly and regulated. We were well dressed and well fed. The yeshivah men were able to resume their studies virtually undisturbed. Their young wives traded recipes and prepared ingenious meals for their husbands. Those *bachurim* who were still single were searching for brides in earnest. They did not have far to look, because there were plenty

---

* The words comprise the twelfth of the Thirteen Articles of Faith, which are part of the daily morning service: "I believe with perfect faith in the coming of the Messiah, and even if he should tarry, I will await his coming every day." The melody was composed by Azriel David Fastag, an adherent of the rabbinic dynasty of Modzhitz, whose melodies are sung by *chassidim* the world over.

of girls from fine families at the B'nos Agudath Israel shelter right there at Zachodnia 66. During our stay in Lodz we helped celebrate many engagements and weddings, which were held in the hall of community headquarters — also at Zachodnia 66.

Postwar Anti-Semitism

PRIOR TO WORLD WAR II, there had been in Poland approximately three and one-quarter million Jews, living together in close-knit communities. In fact there were many cities where the Jews had formed the majority of the population.

After the Holocaust, only one hundred thousand Jews survived in Poland. These were joined by approximately another one hundred thousand Polish Jews who were repatriated from Russia, making Poland's total postwar Jewish population no more than two hundred thousand. Hardly any Jews were ready to reestablish their homes in Poland, where millions of Jews had been brought to death with the help of a great part of the Polish population, and these survivors made no secret·of their plans to go elsewhere.

Yet even the sad remnant that had lived to return to Poland

seemed too much for the Polish populace. Instead of showing us sympathy, the Poles, if anything, were even more hostile than they had been before the coming of Hitler. The Polish anti-Semites were further incited by vicious lies and propaganda spread by certain members of the Polish Catholic clergy. Much of the gentile hatred now was based on crude self-interest. The Poles had taken to themselves all the belongings left behind by the Jews who had been deported. They lived in fine houses formerly owned by Jews, and ate and drank from beautiful china, crystal and silver they had stolen from the Jews. I myself once saw a beautiful *b'somim* box (Havdalah spice box) at the home of a Polish gentile. Naturally, the Poles had no intention of returning these precious articles to their rightful owners or their heirs.

Looking for Ways to Emigrate

ANTI-SEMITISM IN POLAND had assumed terrifying dimensions. Young gentiles would stop trains, seize Jewish passengers and drag them to the woods near the tracks, where they shot them. These incidents only increased our desire to leave Poland. Many Jews crossed the Polish border into Czechoslovakia, from where they smuggled themselves into West Germany. Once in the West, they made contact with *B'richa*, an underground organization that helped bring Holocaust survivors to Eretz Yisrael illegally, in the face of Britain's harsh restrictions against Jewish immigration to Palestine. But most of us yeshivah *bachurim* were not courageous enough to take such risks and so we remained in Lodz, waiting impatiently for a safer opportunity to leave Poland.

We began to organize ourselves. By that time former students and teachers of several yeshivah communities had arrived in Lodz and reconstituted themselves into groups according to the yeshivos they had attended or led before the war. A committee was set up, consisting of two representatives from each yeshivah community, to find ways of speeding our departure from Poland. Rabbi Yosef Nevenansky and I represented the yeshivah of Kletzk; Rabbis Dovid Zaritzky and Sholom Shurpin, the yeshivah of Radin; Rabbis Sholom

Lebowitz and Tuvia Goldstein, the yeshivah of Kamenetz; Rabbis Israel Mowshowitz and Yehuda Leib Nekritz, the yeshivah of Bialystok, and Rabbis Henoch Piotrokowsky and Leib Ziviak, all the students from Polish yeshivos. Our committee met twice each week to discuss its activities. We were in touch with rescue organizations in Europe and America, and received much help and moral support from Mrs. Recha Sternbuch, an Orthodox underground-rescue activist in Zurich who, together with her husband, had saved thousands of Jewish lives during the Holocaust years.*

Rabbi Zuckerman gave me the task of registering all the yeshivah students and their wives for the records of the Polish government and the files of the Vaad Hatzalah. This I did most happily, using a corner of Rabbi Zuckerman's apartment as my office with a tiny table as my desk.

---

* Their story is told in *Heroine of Rescue*, by Joseph Friedenson and David Kranzler, Mesorah Publications, 1984.

My Search for the Fischermans

SOON AFTER RIVKA AND I had settled in our quarters at Zachodnia we became anxious about Rivka's family, whom we had left aboard the train when we got off at Lodz.

First of all, we had to find out where the repatriation train from Kazakhstan had made its last stop. After many inquiries (communications were still in a chaotic stage), we learned that the train, after leaving Lodz, had proceeded south in the direction of Breslau, a German city which had been ceded to Poland and renamed Wroclaw. Rivka and I decided that I should travel to Wroclaw. Even if the Fischermans were not there, I might meet other repatriates who would know where they had gone.

I started my journey on a Tuesday afternoon early in June, 1946. As the train began to move, I recited the Traveler's Prayer that all observant Jews say when they set out on a journey, beseeching G-d for protection against enemies, robbers and wild beasts. This time I recited the prayer with particular intensity because traveling in those days of uncertain political conditions and anti-Semitic outrages entailed considerable danger. My wife agreed to my making the trip solely because we considered it a *sh'lichus shel mitzvah*, an errand to perform a good deed, and tradition teaches us that one who goes on such a journey will come to no harm.

The train, which was packed with passengers, took a whole night to make the journey. There were two unscheduled stops, which made me feel a little uneasy, but the train and I arrived safely in Wroclaw at eight o'clock the next morning.

My first problem was where I could put on my *tefillin* and recite my morning prayers. The station was crowded with Germans and Poles, and I feared that I might endanger my safety if I attracted their attention. Eventually I found a secluded corner in the station where I believed I would not be observed. I quickly put on my *tefillin* and recited the *shema*. Then I removed my *tefillin*, completing my prayers without them. Afterwards, I sat down on a bench and ate my breakfast, a bread-and-butter sandwich my wife had put into my little suitcase.

The Fischermans in Wroclaw

LATER, I FOUND in the station several Jews who told me that they were repatriates from Russia. I asked them whether they knew anything about the Fischerman family. They said that they knew most of the Jewish repatriates in Wroclaw but that the name Fischerman was not familiar to them. They suggested that I go to the market place in the center of the city where many people came not only to do business but to exchange news. Perhaps someone there might have news of the Fischermans.

The center of the city was some distance from the station, and since public transportation had not yet been restored, I had to walk all the way. This gave me ample opportunity to see the destruction wrought by the Allied bombing. Buildings lay in ruins and wide avenues were piled high with debris. The Germans I passed in the streets exuded an air of defeat, nervousness and dejection. They were shabbily dressed and offered all kinds of articles as barter for a piece of bread. The obsequious manner in which they bowed and addressed me as *"Gnädiger Herr"* (Gracious Sir) filled me with disgust.

The central market place of Wroclaw was a huge open space, crowded with people — Germans, Poles and Jews. I walked about for an hour looking for a familiar face. Lo and behold, just as I was about to give up in frustration, such a face appeared. It was Rivka's brother, Tzvi Fischerman. After we had embraced, he asked me what on earth had made me come to Wroclaw. I told him, and he took me to the house where my parents-in-law and the other Fischermans were staying. I spent two days with them in Wroclaw and then returned to Lodz. We never lost touch with Rivka's family again. Eventually Rivka's parents, two of her brothers and one sister settled in Israel. Other members of the family settled in Montevideo, Uruguay.

Distinguished Visitors

SINCE IT SEEMED that we might have to stay in Lodz indefinitely, we were determined to make the best of it. Eventually, all the married couples moved out of Zachodnia 66 and found apartments of their own. Actually, each "apartment" was only a fraction of a room, because in most cases one room was shared by three yeshivah couples. Rivka and I moved into such a place. It certainly was not the happiest arrangement, but there was no alternative.

In each room there was one stove on which all the tenants cooked. Since potatoes were cheap, our diet consisted mostly of potatoes or of foods made from potatoes: potato soup, potato latkes and potato kugel. And while our wives kept house for us, we men spent our days at study.

Rabbi Eliezer Silver in Lodz, Poland in 1946, with a group of survivors

One morning at the synagogue we were surprised to see a bearded Jew dressed in the uniform of an American army officer. We wondered whether the American army had Jewish officers with full beards. We quickly discovered that the officer was none other than Rabbi Eliezer Silver of Cincinnati, Ohio, the saintly leader of the Vaad Hatzalah in the United States. He had come to Poland to visit communities of Holocaust survivors, to see what might be done for them. Since it was considered dangerous for a bearded Jew to walk through the streets of Poland, the American authorities had given Rabbi Silver special permission to wear the uniform of a brigadier general in the United States Army.

Rabbi Silver's visit filled us with new hope and courage. First, he did what any distinguished rabbi might be expected to do when visiting a yeshivah community; he delivered a learned discourse on a Talmudic theme: certain aspects of the sacrifices offered in the Temple in Jerusalem. But then he made a rousing speech from a balcony of Zachodnia 66 to an audience of hundreds in the street below. He thanked us for being so patient with our American Jewish rescuers and assured us that the leaders of Orthodox Jewry in the United States, through Vaad Hatzalah, were doing everything in their power to speed our departure from Poland.

In view of the anti-Semitic atmosphere, a Jewish outdoor rally such as the one addressed by Rabbi Silver might have courted trouble, but it seems that the Poles had too much respect for Rabbi Silver's American uniform to dare molest his listeners.

Another important visitor to our repatriate community came from Eretz Yisrael. He was Binyamin Mintz, a well-known Orthodox journalist and leader of Po'ale Agudath Israel (the labor wing of the Agudath Israel movement), who had left Poland for Palestine long before the war and was a member of the Rescue Committee of the Jewish Agency. Like Rabbi Silver, Reb Binyamin promised us that our fellow Jews in the free world would not let us down.

WE WERE HAPPY to know that our religious leaders in America and Eretz Yisrael were not sitting with their hands folded but

Encouraged were using every possible means to help us leave.

No history of Jewish rescue activities during World War II and its aftermath can be complete without a reference to the work of Recha Sternbuch in Zurich. To her, kindness was not just a *mitzvah*, an act to be performed for duty's sake, but a part of her very being. She was convinced that since it had been G-d's will that she should live in the safety of neutral Switzerland, it was her duty to help those Jews who were not as fortunate as she herself had been. During the war, she negotiated with the Germans to barter Jews for money and in countless instances she succeeded in saving Jewish lives. After the war she devoted her energies to making certain that those Jewish children who had survived the Holocaust in homes and shelter run by gentiles should not be lost to Judaism. Thus, soon after the war, Mrs. Sternbuch, accompanied by the Polish Agudah leader Shimon Zuker,* turned

---

* Mr. Zuker hailed from Lodz. He survived the Nazi death camps, and lived in New York City. In his determination to keep the memory of the martyred Jews alive, Mr. Zuker founded Zacher Institute and compiled *The Unconquerable Spirit*, published by Mesorah Publications in 1980, a short time before his passing.

DISTINGUISHED VISITORS / 131

up one day in the Polish resort town of Zakopane. There, Mrs. Sternbuch and Mr. Zuker headed straight for a gentile children's home where they knew that over three hundred orphaned children from Orthodox Jewish families were still kept, probably in hopes that they could be weaned away from their Judaism and converted to Christianity. Sternbuch and Zuker suggested to the administrators of the home that their Jewish charges might enjoy a day's hike in the nearby mountains. But instead of bringing the children back to the home the next day, the two rescue workers provided them with forged passports and smuggled them out of Poland. By the time the police started searching the countryside for the three hundred missing children, the children and their "abductors" had left the Polish border behind them and were well on their way to Western Europe.

During the period immediately following the war, Mrs. Sternbuch visited Lodz several times as a representative of the Vaad Hatzalah in the United States. It was she who disbursed the funds sent from America to pay for the maintenance of Zachodnia 66, the meals for the unmarried yeshivah *bachurim* and the weekly stipends for the yeshivah couples. It was Mrs. Sternbuch, too, who helped work out a plan for getting the yeshivah students out of Poland.

The plan entailed our obtaining three-month transit visas for Czechoslovakia, in return for a guarantee that we would not attempt to seek permanent residence there. Instead of each individual receiving a personal visa, we were to receive collective visas, each visa covering a group of one hundred rabbis and rabbinical students. In this way, with a little bribery and flattery, the Polish border officials could be persuaded not to count heads too carefully, so that the number of Jews leaving Poland on each visa could be a good deal more than one hundred.

Like many of her co-workers, Mrs. Sternbuch was humble to the point of self-effacement, so that most of us never met her and could never thank her for helping us in the rebuilding of our lives.

Exodus from Poland

IN THE MORNING OF JULY 4, 1946 we were horrified to hear that there had been a pogrom in the town of Kielce. Polish hooligans had murdered forty-five Jews, many of whom had survived the German death camps. We were shocked and heartbroken, and the day on which the victims were buried was a day of deep mourning in our yeshivah community.

During those turbulent days I myself once had a narrow escape from death. Two friends and I were standing on the sidewalk outside Zachodnia 66, talking. I stood facing the street and my two friends, when a horse-drawn carriage containing two passengers passed by. I paid no attention to it until I saw to my horror that one of the passengers was pointing a rifle straight at me. Instinctively, I jumped aside just as the gun went off. The bullet hit a wall in front of which I had stood only seconds before. My friends and I ran into the courtyard of Zachodnia 66, trembling from head to foot, and resolved to use any means, legal or illegal, to leave Poland.

It seems that the tragedy in Kielce helped speed the rescue efforts of our fellow Jews in America, for only two weeks later we received the long-awaited news that a train would leave from Katowice for Prague on Sunday, July 28. We were given instructions to report at the Katowice railroad station (several hundred kilometers from Lodz) at eleven o'clock that morning. We were beside ourselves with joy and gave thanks to G-d for His help and for His messenger, Recha Sternbuch.

Since we had to be in Katowice early on Sunday morning, we

*In Lodz,
Rabbi Brizman, ז״ל (l.)
and Rabbi Shmuel Orenstein*

had to leave Lodz before Shabbos. The one train that went from Lodz to Katowice before the end of that week left Lodz on Wednesday, July 24. And so we took leave of our friends who could not yet go and happily put Lodz behind us. We arrived in Katowice that evening. Meanwhile, in Lodz, despite the departure of most of the students, the yeshivah still continued to operate under the leadership of Rabbi Shmuel Orenstein, now a *rav* in Manhattan, Rabbi Zvi Tanenbaum, now a *rav* in Boston, and Rabbi Glazerman.

We spent Thursday walking through the town. We also visited Rivka's youngest brother, Yehoshua, a boy of thirteen, who, largely due to my efforts, had been accepted at an Agudath Israel children's home in the nearby town of Vitom. When he saw us, he cried bitterly and begged us to take him away from the home, but we comforted him with the assurance that as soon as his parents had firm plans for the future, he would be reunited with them and the rest of the family.

WE SPENT THAT SHABBOS in Sosnowice, a town not far away, where there were more Jews than in Katowice. Morning services **Sosnowice** at the synagogue were well attended and were followed by *Kiddush* and a fine dinner at the home of a family that had returned to the town from the death camps. That afternoon, we were invited to eat *sholosh seudos*, the third Sabbath meal, with yet another family of concentration camp survivors. Both meals were enhanced by good company and lively singing. It was a Shabbos not unlike the Sabbath we had known at home before the war, and we felt as if the intervening years had never been.

On Sunday morning we reported at the Katowice railroad station, where we were met by representatives of the Vaad Hatzalah. With prayers of thanksgiving in our hearts, we boarded the train that was to take us to Prague. The train pulled out of the station at noon.

After an hour's ride due south, our train came to an abrupt stop in an open space. However, we were not surprised or alarmed, because we could see that this was the Czech border. The

A Chanukah celebration in 1946 at Viton, the orphanage established by Recha Sternbuch. At the center is Rabbi Yitzchok Liebes, to his r. is Rabbi Shmuel Orenstein.

EXODUS FROM POLAND / 135

Vaad Hatzalah representative who had traveled with us until this point got off the train and handed the list of names of the collective visa to the Czech immigration officials. We stood at the window of our car and watched the negotiations, which took only ten minutes.

After that, our train continued its journey into Czech territory without anyone counting or verifying the number of people listed on our collective visa.

Prague

WHEN OUR TRAIN made its first stop on Czechoslovakian soil and took on passengers bound for Prague, we noticed a striking difference between the Poles we had left behind and the Czechs we now saw for the first time. While the Poles had looked at us with undisguised malice, the Czechs showed us respect and sympathy. Among the passengers was a middle-aged man, the principal of a high school in Prague. When he heard that we were Jews who had spent the war years in Siberia and Kazakhstan, he asked us whether he could help us in any way and assured us that we could count on the sympathy and good will of the Czech populace. However, he suggested that we not speak Yiddish in public because it sounded so much like German that the Czechs might attack us, thinking that we were Germans!

In Prague we were met by a reception committee and distributed among the various hotels of the city. Rivka and I found ourselves in the hotel called Regina. The plush carpeting and elegant furniture told us that this was an expensive place and that we probably would not be permitted to stay there very long.

We were not mistaken. Within a very short time we were moved to a somewhat plainer hotel, the Stara Posta, where we found many of our friends from Lodz.

We spent the next several days strolling through the Old City and riding through Prague on trolley cars that were new and immaculate. We visited the nine bridges that crossed the Moldau river. We were particularly distressed by one bridge on which there was a crucifix, bearing the Hebrew inscription *kodosh, kodosh, kodosh* ("Holy, holy, holy") and the Hebrew letters of the ineffable name of G-d. We later learned the story of this strange combination. In 1690, the Jewish community of Prague had been forced to add, and pay for, the Hebrew inscriptions on that crucifix, supposedly because one Jew in Prague had made insulting comments about the cross of Christianity. We yeshivah *bachurim* were pained at the inscriptions, which we considered desecrations of the Name of G-d.

On Shabbos morning, we went to *daven* at the famous *Maharal* synagogue, named for the legendary R. Yehuda Loeb ben Bezalel. The *Mussaf* service was led by a fine cantor, Sholom Katz, who had survived the death camps and eventually settled in the United States.

Within three weeks, the refugee committee that saw to our needs rented a building in Diablice, a suburb of Prague, for our yeshivah community. Each of the married couples received a room of its own. One large hall was used for prayer and study. Before long, the chant of Torah study could be heard in our study hall throughout the day and much of the night.

Once again, Rabbi Eliezer Silver came to visit us. This time, he asked to see my brother Berl and me alone in his hotel suite. It turned out that before settling in Cincinnati, Rabbi Silver had been the Orthodox rabbi in Harrisburg, Pennsylvania, where an aunt and uncle of mine, the Zuckermans, had been among his

Rabbi Mishkowski walking with a group of survivors in Diablice

From l. to r. The Boyaner Rebbe, Rabbi Eliezer Silver, the Kopyczynitzer Rebbe

138 / FROM KLETZK TO SIBERIA

Rabbi Isaac Halevi Herzog

most devoted supporters. Rabbi Silver handed us some money, which he said the Zuckermans had asked him to give us.

Rabbi Silver was not only a prince of Torah learning but also great in good works. He spent all his time in Prague distributing money among needy Jews. There was always a long line of people waiting for Rabbi Silver in the lobby outside his room, and no one left emptyhanded. Later, when we met again in New York, Rabbi Silver shyly admitted that much of the money he had distributed among the refugees had not come from philanthropic organizations but from his personal funds.

ANOTHER DISTINGUISHED VISITOR to our yeshivah community in Prague was Rabbi Dr. Isaac Halevi Herzog, the chief rabbi of **Rabbi Isaac Halevi Herzog** Eretz Yisrael. He brought with him his son Jacob, a Torah scholar in his own right who was to hold a high position in the government of the State of Israel before his untimely death. A delegation of yeshivah *bachurim* met with the visitors, who assured them that everything possible was being done to bring us out of Europe. Rabbi Herzog also delivered a Talmudic discourse at the *Maharal* synagogue; it dealt with the laws to be observed when the Temple in Jerusalem will be rebuilt.

The yeshivah in Prague. Seated (l. to r.) are Rabbis Yitzchok Makowski (Brooklyn), Israel Karpel (Israel), Chiel Nisselbaum (Brooklyn), Mordechai Londinsky (Israel), Avrohom Tropp ז"ל (Brooklyn), Victor Vorhand (Manhattan), Leib Greenspan ז"ל (Brooklyn), Michel Shishko ז"ל (Brooklyn),Elinson (Israel), D. Mishkowski (Israel), Yaakov Yosef Morgenstern (Caracas, Ven.), Mordechai Oreizenshtok (Chicago), Hirsh Wiener ז"ל (Brooklyn), Leib Silverstein ז"ל (Brooklyn). Standing (l. to r.), Rabbis Beinush Bernstein (Bronx), Zundel Gulburth (Brooklyn), Berl Chaifec (Boston), Chonon Bondner (Israel), Yitzchok Leib Cipkin (Brooklyn), Lipa Salomon (Boston), Pinchas Kozlovski (Bronx), Israel Portnoy (Brooklyn), Kalman Halpern (Bronx), Chaim Plotnik (Brooklyn), Yosef Brisker (Brooklyn)

A group of survivors in Prague with Rabbi Mishkowski

Among others who made contact with our yeshivah community was Rabbi Chizkie Yosef Mishkowski, the rabbi of Krinki, one of Poland's most famous rabbinical figures, who came to us with his son David. Reb Chizkie was like a father to the individual yeshivah *bachurim*, helping them with food, clothing and sound advice.

Two friends from the United States who visited us were Rabbi Boruch Faskowitz, a prominent yeshivah educator, and Mr. Leo Gartenberg, who became well known as the owner of a large Orthodox Jewish resort in the Catskills. After talking to these gentlemen we felt that G-d had indeed decided that our troubles should come to an end.

Our first official business in Prague was to obtain Polish passports, without which we could not receive American immigration visas. We got these passports without much difficulty from the Polish consulate in Prague, but when we presented them to the American consulate to have our U.S. visas stamped into them, we were told that the demand for the visas was so great that it might take months before we could leave for the United States.

This disappointment placed my wife and me into a difficult situation. Rivka was in her final months of pregnancy. If our child would be born before our arrival in the United States, we would need a separate passport and visa for the baby. With all the red tape involved, we feared that we might then be stranded in Prague for years.

Luckily, thanks to the contacts of Rabbi Victor (Zev Zvi), Vorhand, presently a Rav in the West Side of Manhattan, the principal Orthodox rabbi of Prague, Rivka and I were among the first to receive American students' visas from the U.S. consulate in Prague. These visas were good for a limited period only, but we were told that once we were in the United States, arrangements could be made to convert them into immigration visas.

Now that we had our passports and our American visas, the problem was how to obtain passage to New York before the visas expired. Commercial air travel between Czechoslovakia and the United States had not yet been established. Boats were

Rabbi Victor Vorhand

overcrowded and reservations had to be made far in advance of each sailing. We also learned to our dismay that it was not possible for us to get our steamship tickets in Czechoslovakia. We could only be able to buy them after our arrival in Paris, the next scheduled stop on our journey.

BECAUSE THE FORMALITIES connected with the next stage of our travels took time, we were still in Prague during the High Holidays. We spent the season of penitence in a solemn mood of repentance and high resolves for the coming year. Having emerged from years of hunger and privation whole in body and mind, we better appreciated the tradition in the Midrash, that has G-d plead with us, *"Pischu li pesach k'chudo shel machat, va'anee eftach lochem pesach k'pischo shel ulom"* (Make Me an opening in your hearts no bigger than the eye of a needle and I will make you an opening as large as the entrance to a palace). On that Rosh HaShanah we promised ourselves to open

High Holy Days in Prague

142 / FROM KLETZK TO SIBERIA

Rabbi Israel Mowshowitz   *Rabbi Naftali Zev Lebovitz*

our hearts to G-d in every aspect of our lives and to help other Jews to do likewise. We were supported in this effort by the inspiring sermons of our mentors, Rabbi Naftali Lebovitz of the yeshivah of Kamenetz, and Rabbi Israel Mowshowitz, of the yeshivah of Bialystok.

On Yom Kippur night, after the conclusion of the *neilah* service we felt so greatly uplifted that we began to dance to a rousing melody composed for the words of the Prophet Jeremiah. "*Chasdei Hashem ki lo somnu, ki lo cholu rachamov*" (The mercies of G-d are endless; His compassion never ceases). We were so much inspired by the relevance of these words in our lives that we danced and danced oblivious of our weakness after the fast, until the *baal tefillah* brought us back to our senses by starting the weekday evening service.

On the day after Yom Kippur we received the good news that we would leave Prague for Paris in five days — on the intermediate Sunday of Sukkos. Our French visas allowed us to stay in France as visitors for an unlimited period, so that we would have no difficulties if for any reason our departure for America — or, in the case of other friends, for Eretz Yisrael — would be delayed.

The festival of Sukkos that year brought us the joy of being able to recite the blessing over a *lulav* and *esrog* for the first time since Sukkos of 1939. We sat in the large *sukkah* that had been set up for our yeshivah community and sang far into the night. However, we had to curtail our *Simchas beis HaShoevah* in the evening after *Shabbos Chol HaMoed*, the intermediate Sabbath of Sukkos, because we were leaving Prague early the next morning.

While our train passed through Germany on its way to Paris, most of us did not get off at any station stops because we felt we would be defiling ourselves by setting foot on German soil. Some could not even bear to look through the windows and see the German faces outside because we saw in every German a murderer of our loved ones.

Paris and London

EARLY ON TUESDAY MORNING, the fourth intermediate day of Sukkos, we arrived in Paris. It was five years to the day since our departure from Labor Camp Number Seven.

In Paris, most of the students were temporarily housed in a mansion that had once been the home of the French Baron Rothschild. There, the *bachurim* celebrated the remainder of Sukkos without even unpacking their belongings.

Rivka and I, along with others who possessed American visas, were placed into a hotel on the Rue de Rose, near the Jewish quarter known as the *Pletzl*. This location had been chosen for us because it was close to the steamship line offices where we had to stand in long lines, returning day after day, waiting for accommodations on a boat bound for New York.

On our first Shabbos in Paris we *davened* in the famous synagogue on Rue de Paris, where we heard a sermon by the rabbi, Shmuel Yaakov Rubinstein, who spoke to us in Yiddish.

That night and again the next day, Simchas Torah, during *hakofos*, we, who had lived through seven years of Communism, danced with French Jews who had survived the German occupation of France. All of us had witnessed miracles during the seven years just past, and we sang, over and over again, "*Netzach Yisrael lo yeshaker*" (Israel's eternity will never fail).

Eventually, the leaders of our yeshivah community managed to rent several buildings in the town of Bailly, fifteen miles outside Paris, as a center for those yeshivah students who were still waiting for visas to the United States or other countries. There, the men studied day and night under the guidance of Rabbis Avrohom Tropp, Naftali Lebovitz, Israel Mowshowitz and Yehudah Leib Nekritz. Reb Mordechai Pogramansky, a survivor of a Lithuanian ghetto, delivered lectures on *mussar* — Jewish ethics and moral conduct. As in Lodz and Prague, so in Bailly, too, our yeshivah community was honored by visits from outstanding scholars of the Torah world. Harav Yechezkel Abramsky came from London, and Harav Yoseph Kahaneman, head of the great yeshivah of Ponevezh in B'nai B'rak, came from Eretz Yisrael. Both rabbis delivered highly erudite Talmudic discourses, along with heartfelt words of encouragement.

I JOINED MY FRIENDS in Bailly at least twice each week for concentrated "learning" sessions. I could not go more often, because

In Bailly, France

I was busy running from one travel agency to another in an effort to secure steamship tickets, which were virtually unobtainable. Rivka and I

At a meeting in Israel, from l. to r. Rabbis Zalman Sorotzkin, Yechezkel Abramsky, Moshe Feinstein, and Eliezer Silver

146 / FROM KLETZK TO SIBERIA

Rabbi Yoseph Kahaneman

Rabbi Yehudah Leib Nekritz observing a Torah class

knew that unless we arrived in New York within five weeks, we would be faced with the necessity of securing a passport and visa for a new member of our family. We were also told that if we did not use our visas within a period of three months after we had received them, the visas would lose their validity. An American visa lost through failure to use it was almost never re-issued. Eretz Yisrael was already as good as closed to "legal" immigrants, and Rivka was in no condition to risk the hardships of traveling with the *B'richa* transport of "illegals." If we lost our chance to go to America, where could we go?

Once again, our beloved Rosh Yeshivah, Reb Aharon Kotler, who knew of our plight, came to our rescue. When Mr. Stephen Klein, a successful businessman (he was the manufacturer of Barton's candies) and active supporter of Orthodox Jewish organizations, came to Paris as a representative of the Vaad Hatzalah, he had instructions from Reb Aharon to do his utmost to obtain passage for us. Mr. Klein contacted us immediately upon his arrival in Paris, and within a week we had two tickets on the *Queen Elizabeth*, which was to leave Southampton, England, on Friday, November 22, 1946. (By that time my brother Berl and his wife also had their American visas and left for the United States aboard another boat.)

Mr. Stephen Klein

Rabbi Zeidel Semiatitzky

In order to meet the *Queen Elizabeth*, Rivka and I had to leave Paris for England on Wednesday. We took the train from Paris to the port of Calais, from which we crossed the English Channel by boat. The crossing took only an hour and a half but was so turbulent that I was violently seasick.

THAT EVENING, we arrived in London aboard the boat train from the Channel port of Dover. From the station in London we immediately telephoned Rabbi Zeidel Semiatitzky, dean of the famous Schneider yeshivah in London. Reb Zeidel immediately dispatched one of his students to the station to bring us to his home, where he and his wife received us most warmly. That evening, the Semiatitzkys and we spent hours exchanging our experiences: they told us what they had gone through during the war and the Nazi *blitz* bombing of London, while we described life as we had seen it under the Communist system.

London on the Way to U.S.A.

The next morning Rabbi Semiatitzky telephoned Rabbi Eli Bloch, a former student of the Kletzk yeshivah who had been a good friend of mine. Bloch had been inducted into the Polish army when the war broke out and had been captured almost

PARIS AND LONDON / 149

immediately by the Germans. He had survived the German prison camps and, after the war, made his way to London (eventually, he moved to the United States, settling in Brooklyn). He came to us almost immediately, and we spent the day together, touring the historical sights of London. We also visited a few Orthodox Jewish leaders, among them Mr. Bakst, a well-known London businessman and son of Reb Aaron Bakst, the last rabbi of Shavli, Lithuania.

Rivka and I had brought with us from Paris a generous supply of groceries, including sugar and salami. As we crossed the Channel we wondered why we had done that. Weren't we going to England, which had won the war? Surely, food would not be scarce in England! Really, I said to Rivka, we must get rid of our wartime mentality; it was no longer necessary to hoard food or to give groceries as gifts to families whose hospitality we would accept.

But after our arrival in London we were glad we had not come emptyhanded. Ironically, a year and a half after the war, Germany, the loser, had enough food for all her population, and France, the Nazi collaborator, even had a surplus, while England, the one victorious power, was in the midst of a severe food shortage. Almost all staples — meat, sugar, salt, oil — were still rationed, and we were happy that we had the salami and sugar to give as gifts to Rabbi and Rebbetzin Semiatitzky. They first refused to take our present, but when we insisted, arguing that we would have little need for the food on the boat and certainly not in America, they accepted it.

ON FRIDAY MORNING, November 22, after saying goodbye to our hosts, we took the train to Southampton, where we boarded

Statue of Liberty

the *Queen Elizabeth*. On board the ship we met a great many old acquaintances, including Rabbi Osher Babad and his wife, who had lived in England for some time and were now emigrating to the United States.

We were delighted to find that, unlike many Jewish refugees who had made the crossing aboard "displaced persons transports," Rivka and I had a cabin all to ourselves. We expected to have a pleasant, comfortable trip. However, the sea was rough and for four of the five days that it took the *Queen Elizabeth* to reach New York I was so seasick that I could not eat anything and spent most of the time lying on my berth. Only on the last day of the crossing did I feel well enough to venture on deck and inhale the clean, brisk ocean air.

Standing on deck on Wednesday, the fifth day of the voyage, we heard someone shouting, "I see land!" As we approached New York harbor, we saw a statue of a woman holding a torch in her outstretched right arm. We asked a sailor standing near us what the statue meant. He explained that this was the Statue of Liberty, America's welcome to all the homeless who had come to build new lives for themselves in the land of freedom. He also told us that there was, inscribed on the pedestal of the statue, a poem by Emma Lazarus. "A Jewish lady, I think, she was," he added. Tears filled our eyes. Was there really a country on this earth where Jews were actually welcome?

Ellis Island

AS SOON AS WE DOCKED in New Yokr Harbor, immigration officers boarded the boat and began to check the papers of each immigrant. Since there were about two thousand such passengers, and each person took about five minutes to be cleared, this procedure took hours.

When our turn finally came, the immigration officer looked at our papers for a long while and then called his superior. There seemed to be a problem with our visas, he said, and we would have to wait on board until everyone else had been "processed."

After the last passenger had left the boat, we were told that the American consul in Prague had made a mistake. Rivka's visa should have been issued to her as the wife of a rabbinical student, namely, myself. Instead, she, too, had been given a student's visa. Since a woman obviously could not be an Orthodox rabbinical student, we would not be allowed on American territory until that error had been rectified. A small boat would pick us up shortly to take us to a place called Ellis Island.

By that time, Rivka and I were close to tears. After all these months of wandering, had we reached America only to be turned back because of one stupid clerical error?

One of the immigration officials took pity on us and asked a colleague, who spoke Yiddish, to explain to us that we had nothing to fear. We would not be sent back to Europe. We would only have to go through some legal procedures that would take a day or two. After that, we would be free to start our lives in America. These sympathetic words calmed us and restored our spirits.

As we stepped onto the pier to transfer from the *Queen Elizabeth* to the Ellis Island ferry, we saw a familiar figure waiting on the dock. It was Rabbi Eliezer Silver; accompanied by a delegation of lay leaders, he had come to meet what was, in fact, the first contingent of Jews from the Siberian labor camps to arrive in the United States. When he saw Rivka and me, he ran toward us. Although this was apparently against immigration rules, the officials did not attempt to restrain him but made it clear that he could not engage in any long conversations with us. "*Sholom aleichem!*" said Rabbi Silver. "Don't worry. Everything will be *b'seder* (just fine)." With that, he pressed a bill into my hand. I looked at it; it was five dollars. I did not accept the money but he insisted. "Take it, children, take it," he said. "You will need it on Ellis Island for drinks and cigarettes." Then with a smile and a wave, he left us.

Berl and Sarah

HALF AN HOUR LATER we arrived on Ellis Island. Ordinarily, as we later learned, we would only have been detained there for a day or two, but because the next day, November 28, was a legal holiday, Thanskgiving Day, we were told that we would have to remain on the island for the entire long weekend, until Monday, December 2.

We met other immigrants who had problems with their passports or visas. In the middle of Thursday night, we were awakened by familiar voices. We looked and, to our immense surprise, saw my brother Berl and his wife Sarah. They had just arrived in New York and found themselves in the same difficulty as we. Their consul had made the same mistake as ours — Sarah had been listed as a yeshivah *bachur* when she should have been listed as his wife! As a result, Berl and Sarah, too, had been sent to Ellis Island.

Rabbi Alter Pekier   *Rabbi Berl Pekier*

Just as we began to wonder what we might be able to eat, especially on Shabbos, several women came to the island, bringing with them kosher meat and other Sabbath delicacies, so that we did not have to go hungry.

On Monday morning, December 2, 1946, (9 Kislev 5707) the four of us were released from Ellis Island and, with the help of G-d, set foot upon the land of hope and promise. After seven long years of wandering more than halfway around the globe, we had found peace and safety.

Irving Bunim

OUR FIRST STOP in New York was the office of the Vaad Hatzalah, where we were given a hearty welcome. From there, we telephoned Reb Aharon Kotler, who was then living on the West Side of Manhattan. My eyes filled with tears when I first heard his voice. He blessed us and wished us success in our new lives.

From Vaad Hatzalah headquarters we were taken to the office of Irving Bunim on West 26th Street in Manhattan. Irving (Yitzchok Meir) Bunim was one of Reb Aharon's closest friends in America. From the moment the Rosh Yeshivah had first stepped on American soil, Mr. Bunim had devoted himself to helping him and the "Beth Medrash Govoha," the yeshivah which Reb Aharon had founded in Lakewood, New Jersey.

Mr. Bunim was active in almost every aspect of organized Orthodox Jewish life, including Vaad Hatzalah (the rescue organization), Torah Umesorah (the National Association of Jewish Day Schools) and, above all, the National Council of Young Israel. One of the most popular figures among Orthodox laymen, he was known for his dynamic, original style and was much in demand as a speaker at fund-raising dinners.

When we arrived at Mr. Bunim's office, he was waiting with drinks for *lechayim*. Then, because I was a student of his friend

Irving Bunim being awarded a Sefer Torah at a Chinuch Atzmai dinner. He is flanked by Martin Klein (l.) and Stephen Klein (r.)

Reb Aharon and we were also among the first survivors of the Siberian labor camps to arrive in New York, Mr. Bunim invited us to his home for our first dinner in America. Rivka and I were driven by car to 135 Eastern Parkway, a wide, spacious avenue in Brooklyn, where the Bunim family then lived.

Mrs. Bunim and the Bunim children did everything possible to help us feel at home in their elegant surroundings. During dinner, which was an exquisite meal, and for quite a while afterwards, the Bunims questioned us about our experiences in Siberia and Kazakhstan and listened to our stories with genuine interest. Later, Mr. Bunim took us to the nearby home of his mother-in-law, Mrs. Martz, where we spent our first night in New York.

The next morning, rested and refreshed, we were served a hearty breakfast. Then it was back to Manhattan and to the home of Reb Aharon Kotler on West Ninety-third Street, where we could finally express our thanks to him in person for all that he had done for us. While eating the delicious lunch served by Rebbetzin Kotler, Rivka and I talked and talked, for the Rosh Yeshivah showed a keen interest in everything that concerned our lives, and lives of the other yeshivah students who had spent the war years in Russia

My original plan had been to settle down with Rivka in the *kollel* for married students and their families in Reb Aharon's Lakewood yeshivah, but we could not do so immediately, because Rivka was due to give birth any moment and in no condition to begin housekeeping. Where to live until after the birth of our child was a problem, since we certainly did not wish to impose on Reb Aharon and the Rebbetzin. But Mr. Bunim came to our aid and installed Rivka and me at the home of his sister, Mrs. Ida Abt, who lived at Fifty-sixth Street in the Boro Park section of Brooklyn. The Abts owned a business in the South, so that they were often away from New York for days and weeks at a time. During the six weeks we spent at the Abt home (our other expenses were paid by the American Jewish Joint Distribution Committee, popularly known among refugees as the "Joint"), we virtually had the house to ourselves.

The Birth of Levi

ON DECEMBER 9, 1946, exactly one week after our "official" arrival in New York, our first child, a boy, was born. We named him Levi, after my father. News of the happy event spread quickly through the Orthodox community, because one of New York's popular Jewish newspapers carried a story about Moshe and Rivka Pekier, who had just arrived in the United States after seven years under the Soviet system and had now given birth to an American baby.

Rivka and I were delighted that our first child was a boy, but I was faced with the problem of arranging a *bris* in a strange country where I had arrived only a week earlier and where I had no relatives to whom to turn. We were told that we did not have to worry about a place for the celebration. Beth Israel, the hospital where the baby was born, had a special room for that purpose. Of course an elaborate meal, such as had been customary on these occasions in Europe before the war, was out of the question, because we were supported entirely by funds from the "Joint." After consulting with Rivka and Berl's wife Sarah, we planned a simple collation of *schnapps* and cake.

I learned that the owner of Clark's, a kosher bakery on the Upper West Side, was a *landsman* of mine from Kletzk. I went there, told him about our happy event and selected one large loaf of honey cake and one of sponge cake. He wished me *mazeltov* and wrapped up the cakes, but when I asked him the price he said that I owed him nothing because the cakes were a present from him. Of course I protested. "Look here," I said, "You can't do that. It's your livelihood, after all." When I insisted on paying, my *landsman* said that I owed him one dollar. Greenhorn though I was, I knew very well that two cakes of the size I had ordered must cost a great deal more than one dollar, but I could protest no more. I paid him the dollar and thanked him most heartily for his kind gesture. Afterwards, I stopped at a liquor store to pick up several bottles of whiskey and then I was on my way downtown to Beth Israel Hospital.

The principal quests at my son's *bris*, aside from Berl and Sarah, were Reb Aharon and Rebbetzin Kotler, Rabbi and Mrs. Zelig Fortman of Far Rockaway (cousins of my mother), Mrs. Stephen Klein (whose husband was still in Paris on Vaad Hatzalah business), and of course Mr. and Mrs. Irving Bunim. Among the newcomers present were Rabbi and Mrs. Simcha Nadborny. Reb Simcha was an old friend from Kletzk, who had spent the war years in Shanghai and had only recently arrived in New York. Twenty-two years later, the Nadbornys were to become our first *mechutanim* when their daughter married the infant whose *bris* they had attended.

At the *bris*, Berl and Sarah acted as *kvatters*, bringing the baby into the *bris* room, and Reb Aharon himself served as *sandak*, holding the baby on his knees while the operation was performed.

After the *mazel-tovs* and good wishes, I was about to invite

Rabbi Zelig Fortman

everyone for my *schnapps* and cake, with apologies that I had been unable to provide the kind of *seudah* (feast) that we had known in Europe, when suddenly I was interrupted by the booming voice of our dear Irving Bunim. "The *simchah shel mitzvah* will take place at the headquarters of the National Council of Young Israel on East Sixteenth Street. Everyone is cordially invited." I was speechless, overcome with emotions of joy and gratitude.

At the Young Israel building we found long tables covered with white tablecloths, and a complete dinner was served. Everyone who had attended the *bris* at the hospital came to the *seudah* and joined in the happy spirit of the occasion.

Through all the years that followed, Rivka and I and our family remained close to Irving and Blanche Bunim. Levi's *pidyon haben* took place at the home of the Abts, with our cousin Horav Zelig Fortman serving as the *Kohen* and Reb Aharon, Rebbetzin Kotler and the Bunims attending as honored guests. The Bunims were present also at Levi's *bar-mitzvah* and eventually at his wedding. Mrs. Bunim died many years ago; Mr. Bunim passed away in 1980. My family and I will always cherish their memory.

WHEN OUR SON LEVI was about a month old, we left New York

for Lakewood, where I spent four years in intensive study at the **Beth Medrash Govoha of Lakewood** kollel. We then returned to New York, where I have spent most of my life in Jewish education, first as the Rabbi of Congregation Medrash Eliyahu in East New York, an old Brooklyn neighborhood, and later as Talmudic lecturer at the prestigious West Side Institutional Synagogue in Manhattan. Levi was followed by four girls, Rochel, Chaya, Cheni and Shulamis. All my children are married now. My son and my sons-in-law have *semichah* (rabbinic ordination). Rivka and I have had the joy of seeing our grandchildren grow up in the Jewish tradition, dedicated to study and the observance of our Torah.

Every day I give thanks to G-d for having kept me alive, brought me to this country and given me the opportunity to serve Him, no longer amidst poverty and hardship, but in joy, comfort and contentment.